THIS LITTLE LIGHT

BLOGLOG: Shelley Miller   11/29/2024—3:08 PM

My beautiful daughter, Rory Anne Miller, aged 16, was shot to death in the early hours of this morning. Also dead are Paula Hernandez, 10 years old, Feliza Lopez, 16, and her unborn child, gunned down on the beach near Paradise Cove, California.

Rory and her friends were making their way through the sand to the coast guard boat where I waited, when they were struck by multiple gunshots fired at close range. I was a witness to their execution. A supporter who was driving our rescue boat captured the shooter.

According to the news, cell phone records indicate that the man who shot these innocent children was contacted by Tom Sharpe, of Calabasas, California, three times in the hour before we arrived. Phone records also show that a call was made from the Malibu beach house where the girls sought refuge to Tom Sharpe's cell phone, approximately fifty minutes before they were killed.

I've read the contents of Rory's blog, twice, and I'm posting this uncensored version in its entirety. I think that is what my daughter would want.

Rory Miller didn't believe in God, but she believed in truth, and honesty, humility and humanity. She was relentless in her questioning of herself, and of our world. She had so much to live for, and so much to give, and will be sorely missed by me, by her father, Sherman Miller, and by all who knew her and loved her.

Rory died in my arms, with the moonlight reflected in her eyes. Her last words were, "Mommy. I. Love."

The Crusaders continue to flood the Santa Monica Pier in celebration of what they call justice. I hope that when the truth is revealed, their calls for God's will to be done will become cries for mercy on us all.

Please share Rory's story.

For Feliza. And Paula. And Rory. And all of the other girls.

Lest we forget.

TO:

Zackery Christmas

FROM:

Dad

DATE:

December 25th, 2019

100 EXTRAORDINARY STORIES OF PRAYER for COURAGEOUS Girls

UNFORGETTABLE TALES OF WOMEN OF FAITH

JEAN FISCHER

SHILOH kidz
An Imprint of Barbour Publishing, Inc.

Cover design by Emma Segal

Interior illustrations by Sumiti Collina, Thais Damiao, Aaliya Jaleel, Wendy Leach, Maria Maldonado, Mona Meslier, Isabel Muñoz, Sonya Abby Soekarno

Published by Shiloh Kidz, an imprint of Barbour Publishing, 1810 Barbour Drive, Uhrichsville, Ohio 44683, www.shilohkidz.com.

Our mission is to inspire the world with the life-changing message of the Bible.

 Member of the
Evangelical Christian
Publishers Association

Printed in China.

06650 1019 DS

CONTENTS

Maya Angelou
{1928-2014}

Prayer Changes Things

Maya Angelou lived a difficult childhood. Her parents had separated and there was trouble at home. Maya went to live with her grandmother in Arkansas, but she faced even more trouble there because she was black. Some people did not accept Maya because of the color of her skin. It all became too much, so she stopped speaking. For five years, Maya refused to say even one word.

When she became an adult, Maya made choices that would not please God. But even then she felt something tugging at her spirit. She wanted Jesus; she wanted to be a Christian. One day while taking a class, Maya read the words "God loves me!" The idea that God cared touched Maya's heart and brought her to her knees. She became a praying woman. "When I pray, something wonderful happens," she said. She discovered that prayer changes things. Maya understood that God heard her when she prayed, and she was grateful.

Slowly, her life began to turn around. As she grew closer to God, Maya became wise about life. She wrote poetry and books, and her words made her famous. With God giving Maya strength and courage, she felt at peace speaking in front of huge crowds, sometimes as large as ten thousand people. In 1993 Bill Clinton asked her to write a special poem for his inauguration as president of the United States, and the world watched on television while Maya recited "On the Pulse of Morning."

Maya Angelou was never afraid of sharing her faith and wisdom with others. She knew that fear keeps people from being the best they can be. She had been a frightened little girl with trouble all around. But thanks to God and prayer, Maya grew up to be a wise, strong, and courageous woman—a Christian!

THe Prayer From THe HearT. . .rIGHT WITH GOD Has MUCH Power.
JAMES 5:16

ANNa
{Luke 2:36-38}

Anna's Special Someone

Anna's story begins sadly. Her husband died seven years into their marriage, leaving Anna young and alone. Anna likely missed hearing her husband's voice and knowing he was there to talk with, so she turned to God. He became her Special Someone.

Anna spent many hours each day talking with God. She got so close to God that she learned to recognize His voice in her heart. For many years, the Jewish people knew her as a prophetess—a woman who spoke the words of God. She shared with them what God told her.

One day when Anna was very old, God sent her to the temple to meet a special baby, His Son, Jesus. When Anna saw the baby, she already knew who He was. She prayed and thanked God for Him. Then Anna spent the rest of her life telling others the Good News. She spread the Word that God sent His Son, Jesus, to earth to save people from sin so they could have forever life in heaven. Anna became the first woman missionary!

Just like Anna, you can talk with God! You don't have to be alone or without anyone to talk with before you decide to pray. God wants to hear from you all the time. You don't even have to speak to Him out loud. You can think your prayers and still know that He hears you. God is interested in everything you say. Nothing is too little or unimportant. Start today. Get in the habit of talking with Him every day all day long.

"THEN YOU WILL CALL UPON ME AND COME AND PRAY TO ME, AND I WILL LISTEN TO YOU."
JEREMIAH 29:12

ANNE ASKEW
{1521-46}

Forgive Them!

O Lord," Anne Askew prayed, "I have more enemies now than there be hairs on my head! Yet, Lord. . .I heartily desire. . .that Thou wilt. . .forgive them that violence which they do." Anne prayed that prayer just minutes before she died.

She lived in a time of change and trouble during the reign of King Henry VIII. The king led the Church of England, and he ruled that anyone who did not obey his church's teachings was an enemy of the kingdom. King Henry arrested people who disobeyed him, and some were put to death.

Anne did not believe what the king's church taught. She believed only what the Bible said. When King Henry ruled that women could not read or teach about the Bible, or anything else that disagreed with his religious ideas, Anne disobeyed. She memorized scripture and taught it to others. She read and talked about the Bible as much as she wanted, and that got her into trouble.

The king's men arrested Anne. They ordered her to take back everything she believed and said about the Bible, but Anne refused. For disobeying King Henry, Anne was tortured and killed—a punishment saved for the king's worst enemies. Just before she died, Henry gave Anne one last chance to deny the Bible, but she wouldn't! Instead, Anne prayed for those who hated her. She followed Jesus' teachings in the Bible when He said, "Respect and give thanks for those who try to bring bad to you. Pray for those who make it very hard for you" (Luke 6:28).

Anne Askew's story is a reminder to pray in the worst of times—and also to pray for and forgive those who hurt us. Is there someone you need to forgive today?

. . . .

"WHEN YOU STAND TO PRAY, IF YOU HAVE ANYTHING AGAINST ANYONE, FORGIVE HIM."
MARK 11:25

GLADYS AYLWARD
{1902-70}

God Knows What You Need

After studying for three months in the missionary society college, Gladys Aylward was told that she wasn't educated enough to become a missionary. No one believed she'd be able to learn the Chinese language, and so the committee couldn't accept her. But young Gladys knew deep in her heart that China was where God wanted her to be.

So Gladys decided to get a job as a housemaid, and she worked to save money for a one-way ticket to China. In 1932 she left Liverpool with an old suitcase full of food and clothing.

For eight years Gladys ran an inn in China where mule team drivers could rest and enjoy a meal. She shared God's Word with them and anyone else who would listen. She also took in orphaned children, and she taught them all about Jesus.

Gladys had more than a hundred orphans in her care when she learned the Japanese army was coming to take over the place where they lived. Gladys was desperate to save the children, so she gathered them up, and they all began walking to a safer place—an orphanage in Sian many miles away.

For twelve days they walked, and Gladys was worn out from leading the kids, but she refused to give up.

When they reached the wide and deep Yellow River, they had no way to cross.

"Ask God to get us across," the children said. "He can do anything!"

Gladys and the children knelt down together and prayed, asking God to help them get across the river.

God heard their prayers. A Chinese officer showed up, and he had boats! Gladys and the children crossed the river safely and arrived in Sian.

What a wonderful story about the power of prayer! Whenever you face a challenge, ask for God's help. He knows what you need even before you ask.

"DO NOT FEAR, FOR I AM WITH YOU. DO NOT BE AFRAID, FOR I AM YOUR GOD.
I WILL GIVE YOU STRENGTH, AND FOR SURE I WILL HELP YOU."
ISAIAH 41:10

MARY MCLEOD BETHUNE
{1875–1955}

A Little Girl's Prayer

Born not long after the Civil War, Mary McLeod Bethune watched her parents struggle to make a life free from slavery. They continued working for their former owner, trying to earn enough money to buy land where the family could grow cotton. When that finally happened, the McLeod family praised God. They trusted He had provided them with freedom to begin a new life.

Mary's mom and dad loved God and raised their seventeen children to love Him too. Prayer was an important part of their lives. Even as a little girl, Mary recognized God's greatness and His ability to answer prayers. Her dream was to read and write, so she asked God to make a way for her to learn. Black children were not allowed in school with white children back then.

When she was ten years old, a school for black children opened in a nearby town. Mary walked miles to go there and learn. God answered Mary's prayer! She grew up to graduate from college and become a teacher. But she wanted more. Mary wanted to provide the best education for all African American children, so she opened a school. At first she had six students. Then more came. And more. Mary's school grew until one day it became a college for African American men and women.

Mary kept praying, and God kept leading her forward. He had great plans for her. For the rest of her life, Mary worked to help African Americans gain equality. Her hard work got the attention of President Franklin D. Roosevelt, who chose her as his adviser to help bring Americans together as equals, whatever the color of their skin.

God has a plan for you too. When you pray, be like Mary. Ask God to guide you wherever you go.

" 'FOR I KNOW THE PLANS I HAVE FOR YOU,' SAYS THE LORD, 'PLANS FOR WELL-BEING AND NOT FOR TROUBLE, TO GIVE YOU A FUTURE AND A HOPE.' "
JEREMIAH 29:11

SAINT BIRGITTA OF SWEDEN
{1303–73}

A Life Dedicated to Prayer

Birgitta had a dream in which she saw Jesus on the cross. Birgitta asked Him, "Who did this to You?" Jesus answered, "All those who despise My love." The dream felt so real to seven-year-old Birgitta that she never forgot it.

Years later Birgitta fell in love with a man named Ulf. They married and lived happily in Sweden with their eight children.

One of Birgitta's relatives, the king of Sweden, asked Birgitta to be lady-in-waiting to his new queen. So Birgitta and her family made the long journey to the castle. After years of service, they went home. But on the way back, Ulf got very sick. Birgitta sat praying for her husband when a bishop appeared. He said, "God has great things for you to do."

Ulf died, leaving Birgitta a widow at age forty-one. She asked Jesus to guide her, and she dedicated her life to quiet prayer. She had more dreams in which Jesus told her things, and often Birgitta passed His messages along to others. Sometimes those messages criticized important people, such as the king, priests, and bishops. Birgitta wasn't afraid to tell them to be better Christians and make a difference in the lives of others. And when France and England went to war, Birgitta sat down with representatives of both sides and tried to solve their problems but was unsuccessful.

Much of what Birgitta tried to do failed, but that didn't stop her from praying and relying on Jesus. She moved to Rome and opened her house to anyone who needed help, especially the sick, homeless, and poor.

In 1391 the Catholic Church made Birgitta the patron saint of Sweden, and in 1999 Pope John Paul II named her one of the patron saints of Europe.

What can *you* do to help others in your school, neighborhood, and community? Ask God what He wants you to do. He'll guide you in the right direction.

I HAVE CALLED TO YOU, O GOD, FOR YOU WILL ANSWER ME. LISTEN TO ME AND HEAR MY WORDS.
PSALM 17:6

ANTOINETTE BROWN BLACKWELL
{1825-1921}

She Dared to Speak Up

Antoinette Brown Blackwell was born in a time when children rarely spoke up unless asked. But when she was eight years old, she dared to say her own prayer aloud during family time when her dad always said the prayers. Her brother asked, "Why did you pray aloud?" Antoinette answered, "I think I am Christian, and why should I not pray?" Antoinette joined her family's church at age nine, and she kept speaking up at church meetings.

She was smart! Antoinette loved learning and was a good student. At age fifteen, she became a teacher. Teaching helped her earn money to follow her dream of attending college to become a minister. Some wondered how she dared even think about that at a time when there were no women ministers. That didn't stop Antoinette! She went to college and earned her degree. But when she tried to preach, some of the men shouted and stamped their feet. Still, Antoinette didn't give up. She wanted to become a pastor and lead a church. She believed that day would come.

Antoinette felt that women, like men, could be leaders, and they had the right to be ministers or anything else. So she began speaking up about women's rights. She joined in with other women seeking equality. She kept speaking up and delivering speeches at women's rights conventions.

The day finally arrived when Antoinette was invited to become pastor of the First Congregational Church in Butler and Savannah, New York. Her dream had come true! That little girl who had dared to pray aloud became the first woman minister in the United States.

Antoinette's story inspired other little girls to become ministers or whatever else they wanted to be—and to be brave enough to pray out loud.

BE HAPPY IN YOUR HOPE. DO NOT GIVE UP WHEN TROUBLE COMES.
DO NOT LET ANYTHING STOP YOU FROM PRAYING.
ROMANS 12:12

Catherine Booth
{1829-90}

Mother of an Army

You've seen the red Salvation Army kettles at Christmastime, and you probably noticed volunteers ringing bells as people dropped money inside. The Salvation Army wouldn't exist were it not for Catherine Booth.

Catherine grew up in England in the 1800s. Her parents taught her to love and trust God. In her teens, Catherine injured her spine, and she had to stay in bed for months. To keep busy, she read books about God. She learned how He wants people to live. The more Catherine read, the more she wanted to tell everyone about Jesus and what He taught. She wanted to preach!

When she became well, Catherine fell in love and married a young preacher named William Booth. Together they not only preached, but they also led others to teach about Jesus. Before long the Booths had more than a thousand volunteer helpers. William called them the "Salvation Army," and Catherine became known as "Army Mother." The army grew and grew! Today the Salvation Army helps people in over a hundred countries around the world.

When she preached, Catherine often talked about prayer. She had learned that prayer requires more than just words. The person who prays needs a close relationship with Jesus. That means trusting and obeying Him. Prayer also requires faith and believing that God owes us nothing but He will give us exactly what we need.

Maybe someday God will lead you to preach, like Catherine, or maybe He has a different plan for you. Pray now and begin asking God what He wants you to do when you grow up. Then trust Him to get you there. It will take time and patience, but don't lose faith. God has something good waiting for you right around the corner.

THE LORD IS NEAR TO ALL WHO CALL ON HIM, TO ALL WHO CALL ON HIM IN TRUTH.
PSALM 145:18

ANNE Bradstreet
{1612-72}

America's First Woman Poet

Close your eyes and imagine yourself living long ago in an English castle. Anne Bradstreet didn't have to imagine. She lived it! Anne was born in a castle in Northampton, England, where her father was a steward for an earl—her dad managed the castle and what went on there. Anne was homeschooled—or you might say "castle schooled"—in languages, music, and dancing. She discovered that she liked to write.

Now, imagine Anne leaving the castle and all its richness behind. When she was sixteen, Anne married a young man named Simon Bradstreet, and they sailed off to America to begin a new life. It was difficult for Anne to adjust. America was brand-new, not much was there, and life was hard. But Anne prayed and trusted that God had led her exactly where He wanted her. She settled into a quiet life as a wife and later a mother of eight.

Anne often wrote poetry about her life. Things were not easy for her, and she had much trouble. Many of her poems were like prayers to God. She struggled to know Him better and understand His ways.

In her lifetime, Anne wrote many poems. Her writing became famous! Today she is remembered as the first woman poet in America. Her poems are taught in schools around the world.

Maybe you are like Anne, more comfortable writing your prayers than saying them. That's okay with God! He hears when you pray aloud, when you pray silently, and even when you think words and write them down.

Try writing a prayer poem to God. You might discover a passion to write. Who knows? Maybe you will be the next great American poet!

WHILE SHE KEPT PRAYING TO THE LORD. . .HANNAH WAS SPEAKING IN HER HEART. HER LIPS WERE MOVING, BUT HER VOICE WAS NOT HEARD.
1 SAMUEL 1:12-13

candace cameron-Bure
{1976-}

God Comes First

You probably know of Candace Cameron-Bure. She stars in Hallmark movies and played a main character in the TV series *Make It or Break It*. Candace has been acting since age five. She started doing commercials. Then, at age ten, she landed a big role on the hit comedy *Full House*. In addition to her acting, Candace is known for her Christian faith.

Candace grew up in a family that didn't talk about God. When she was twelve, another family asked hers to attend church. At first church seemed strange to her, but as she continued to attend, Candace felt a change. She was happier. Her heart felt warm inside when she welcomed Jesus in, and Candace became excited about her new Christian life.

When she grew up and got busier, Candace made God less of a priority in her life. When she did things she knew displeased Him, she simply asked for His forgiveness and moved on. But then Candace learned something important. She couldn't just believe in God but then do whatever she wanted, living her life however she thought was right. She needed to live the way He wanted her to live. Candace got on her knees and told God that she wanted to live her life for Him and that she wanted to become the woman He created her to be.

Today Candace makes God her first priority. She does her best to live in ways pleasing to Him, and she is never shy about sharing her faith.

Like Candace Cameron-Bure, you aren't perfect—no one is—but just like her, you can ask God to help you live to please Him.

IF WE STAY HERE ON EARTH OR GO HOME TO HIM, WE ALWAYS WANT TO PLEASE HIM.
2 CORINTHIANS 5:9

Barbara BUSH
{1925–2018}

First Lady

Barbara Pierce Bush is remembered as the wife of former president George H. W. Bush. She was also the mother of President George W. Bush.

Faith in God was important to Mrs. Bush and her husband. They raised their children in a Christian home and made sure they understood how God wanted kids, *and* grown-ups, to behave. The president and Mrs. Bush often prayed together. They were known as world leaders; still they behaved as every Christian should by serving others. They taught Sunday school in their church and helped with their church's outreach ministries.

Barbara Bush did her best to put God first in her life. Some people thought of the president of the United States as all-powerful, but Mrs. Bush knew better. She said, "You may think the president is all-powerful, but he is not. He needs a lot of guidance from the Lord."

Faith and prayer helped Barbara Bush through hard times. When her husband was a young navy pilot, his plane went down. He almost died while waiting to be rescued. Then Barbara's mother died in a car accident, and not many years later the Bushes' young daughter, Robin, died of cancer. The stress was enough to cause Barbara Bush's hair to turn white but not for her to lose faith in God. He carried her through and made her an even stronger wife, mother, and First Lady.

You might think Mrs. Bush was afraid of dying after losing people she loved, but she said, "I'm a huge believer in a loving God. And I don't have a fear of death. . .because I know that there is a great God." She died in 2018 at age ninety-two. George, her husband of seventy-three years, was there holding her hand.

PLEASING WAYS LIE AND BEAUTY COMES TO NOTHING,
BUT A WOMAN WHO FEARS THE LORD WILL BE PRAISED.
PROVERBS 31:30

THE CanaaniTe WOMan
{MaTTHeW 15:21-28}

Patience, Please

Dogs love sitting near their people at dinnertime. If dogs are patient, maybe their owners will give them a bite of food. Think about that as you read the Canaanite woman's story.

Jesus loved everyone, but His priority while on earth was to save the Jewish people from sin. Eventually *everyone* could be saved from sin because of Jesus, but the Jews were first.

The Canaanite woman was not Jewish; still she believed in Jesus' power and love. She had a very sick daughter, and she felt certain Jesus could make her child well again. So she asked for His help.

Jesus' reaction might surprise you. He ignored her when she called out to Him. She kept on calling. Then she went to Him and got on her knees and prayed: "Lord, help me!" Jesus' answer was not what you would expect. He said, "It is not right to take children's food and throw it to the dogs" (vv. 25-26). He meant it wasn't right for Him to give to her what was meant for the Jews. He tested the woman's faith. Would she give up on Jesus because of what He said?

The Canaanite woman replied, "Lord. . .even the dogs eat the pieces that fall from the table of their owners" (v. 27). She knew she was not Jesus' first priority, but still she believed He would give her what she wanted. The woman's strong faith pleased Jesus, and He healed her daughter right away.

Sometimes when you pray, God will ask you to be like the Canaanite woman, to be like a patient dog at a dinner table. He wants you to wait and hold on to your faith, continuing to believe in Him.

Think about it: Are you good at waiting?

LearN WeLL HOW TO WaiT SO YOU WILL Be STrONG aND COMPLETE aND IN NeeD OF NOTHING.
JAMES 1:4

AMY CARMICHAEL
{1867–1951}

Brown Eyes

When Amy Carmichael was little, she asked God to make her brown eyes blue. Amy felt disappointed when it didn't happen, until her mother explained that *no* is sometimes God's answer. She said God has a good reason for every answer, even if His answer is no. He has a purpose for everything He does.

God's love grew in Amy's heart, and so did her need to serve others. As a teenager, she saw girls her age who needed hope. These girls, known as "the shawlies," worked in flour mills in Belfast, Ireland, where Amy lived. They needed to know Jesus, so Amy taught them.

Amy's service didn't end there. She wanted to be a missionary, but she wondered if she should. She prayed, and God said, "Go!" So Amy went—first to Japan and later to India.

In India many girls came to Amy to learn about Jesus. More came, kids of all ages, kids without families who needed a home. Before long Amy had more than fifty children to care for! It was hard work, but God provided Amy everything she needed.

Young girls in India were often kidnapped and used in evil ways, so Amy helped hide them. She disguised herself to look like an Indian woman. Most had brown eyes, just like hers. Amy's brown eyes helped her to blend in among the people instead of standing out. Amy finally understood why God had given her brown eyes instead of blue!

What did you learn from Amy's story? God will always answer your prayers. When the answer is no, you can trust that He has a good reason—He has something even better in His plan for you.

TRUST IN THE LORD WITH ALL YOUR HEART, AND DO NOT TRUST IN YOUR OWN UNDERSTANDING. AGREE WITH HIM IN ALL YOUR WAYS, AND HE WILL MAKE YOUR PATHS STRAIGHT.
PROVERBS 3:5-6

Catherine of Siena
{1347-80}

The Quiet Place

Catherine was born in 1347, the youngest of twenty-five children. Can you imagine the noise and busyness in her house? Like other little children, Catherine was a happy child, but more than anything she appreciated being alone somewhere she could pray. She thought of Jesus as her closest friend.

When Catherine became a teenager, the world around her had changed. Nations and cities fought each other. Peace had gone away. There was even trouble in her home.

Catherine and her parents had a huge disagreement. They wanted her to marry, but she didn't want to. Catherine rebelled. As punishment, her parents gave her chores to do. They didn't allow her what she wanted most, to be alone and pray. Still that didn't stop Catherine from talking with God. He showed her there was a quiet, private place in her heart where she could be with Him.

Her parents finally let Catherine live as she chose. She went into her room and stayed there alone, praying. For three years she didn't leave her room except to attend church! Then God told Catherine to go out and serve others.

She served her family with love. Catherine also taught about Jesus, gave advice to help solve problems, cared for the sick, and helped the poor. She wrote letters to heads of cities and nations and to leaders of the church, begging them to be at peace with each other. Some of her letters still exist.

No matter how busy Catherine got, she always had a quiet place in her heart where she could be alone with Jesus. Did you know that, like Catherine, you also have a quiet place in your heart where you can be alone with Jesus? Ask Him to show it to you.

I pray that Christ may live in your hearts by faith.
I pray that you will be filled with love.
Ephesians 3:17

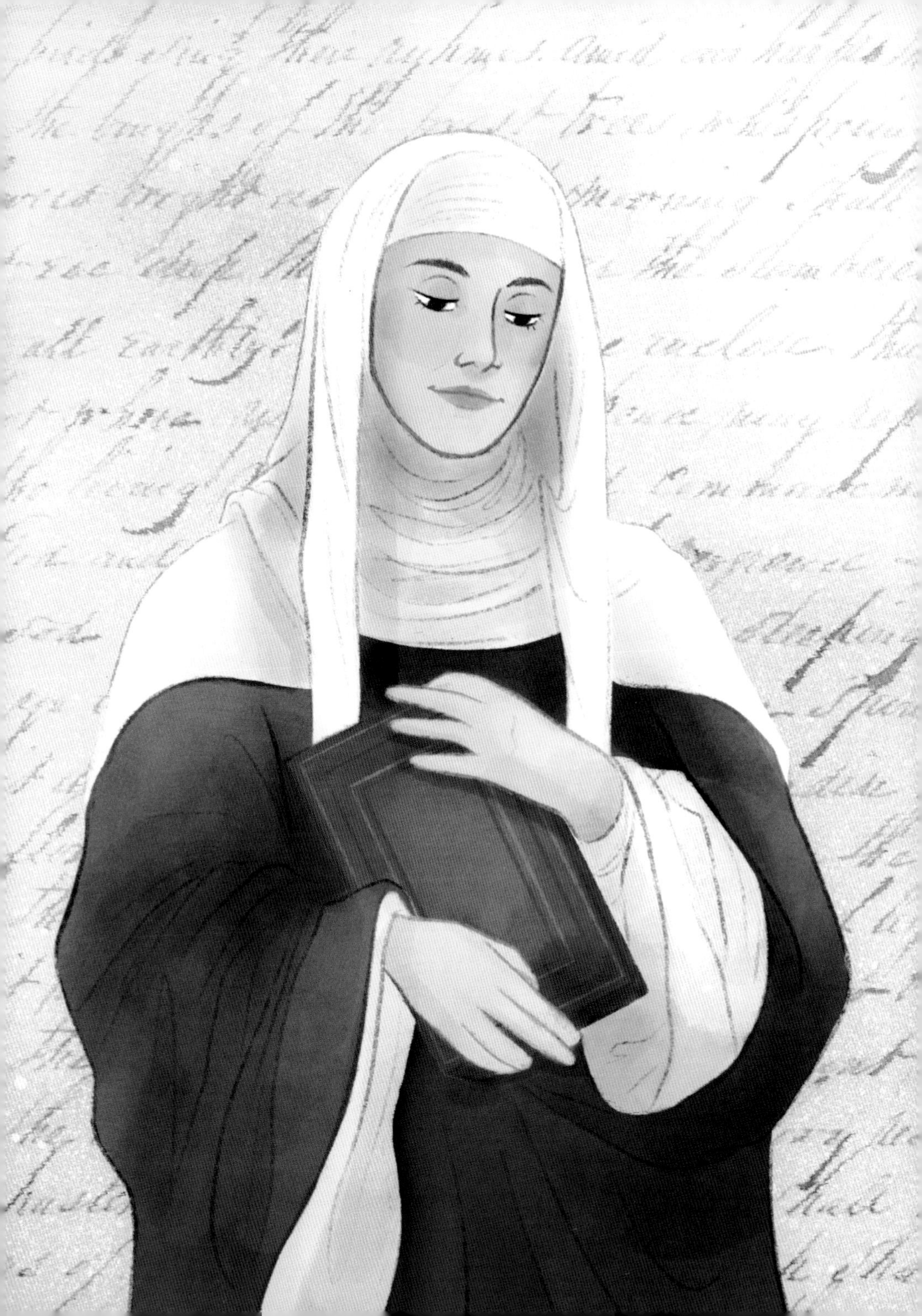

Kelly Clark
{1983–}

She Knocked on the Right Door

When you hear the name Kelly Clark, you think Olympian snowboarder, winner of Olympic medals—and Christian! How Kelly became a Christian is the best part of her story.

At the age of eighteen, Kelly had reached her goals. She was famous! Along with fame came friends and partying. Kelly seemed to have everything, but she felt lost and unloved. *Now what?* she wondered.

Another snowboarder, a Christian named Natalie McLeod, wrote Kelly's name in her prayer journal. She prayed, "Jesus, I ask that You would save this person." Kelly had no idea Natalie was praying for her.

One day while traveling, Kelly overheard a woman comforting a friend who fell and didn't qualify for the finals. "Hey! God still loves you," the woman said.

When Kelly got to her hotel room, she found a Bible and began reading. She needed help understanding it. The woman Kelly had overheard was staying at the same hotel. So Kelly went to her room and knocked on the door. "I think you might be a Christian," she said, "and I think you need to tell me about God." With that woman's help, Kelly gave her life to Jesus.

Life changed for Kelly. She stopped partying and worrying about what came next. She knew God had a purpose for her life. A few months later, Kelly discovered Natalie McLeod had prayed for her. It all made sense then. God had led Kelly to overhear the conversation between two friends, and He also led her to knock on that woman's door and ask about God.

Today Kelly openly shares her Christian faith. You'll see a sticker on her snowboard that says JESUS, I CANNOT HIDE MY LOVE.

Remember, when you pray for someone, God hears. Who will you pray for today?

"ASK, AND WHAT YOU ARE ASKING FOR WILL BE GIVEN TO YOU. LOOK, AND WHAT YOU ARE LOOKING FOR YOU WILL FIND. KNOCK, AND THE DOOR YOU ARE KNOCKING ON WILL BE OPENED TO YOU."
MATTHEW 7:7

Nadia Comaneci
{1961-}

Prayer Makes You Strong

In 1976, at age fourteen, Nadia Comaneci became the first woman ever to score a perfect ten in Olympic gymnastics. Four years later, she won two gold medals in the Olympics. Little girls all over the world who loved gymnastics wanted to be like Nadia. But there was a dark side to her story.

She grew up in Romania, a Communist country, where prayer was not allowed. Nadia's family believed in God. Her grandmother taught her to kneel and pray each night, and God became important to Nadia.

As a young woman in her early twenties, Nadia retired from Olympic sports. She worked in Romania to support herself and her family, but her pay was hardly enough to heat the house and put food on the table. The government watched Nadia closely. They worried she might decide to leave Romania for a better life in the United States. To do that would be daring and enough to put Nadia in jail if she was caught.

Nadia decided to go! She escaped on a cold winter night. Walking in darkness, Nadia relied on prayer and God to get her to safety. She prayed that the government wouldn't turn against her family because she ran away. With God's help, she reached the US embassy in Austria and from there went to the United States. In the United States, Nadia was free to work and send money to her family in Romania.

Today Nadia's favorite quote is: "Don't pray for an easy life; pray to be a strong person." Nadia prays all the time.

Think about Nadia's story and remember that prayer makes you strong. Whatever trouble you face, God is with you—but don't just pray when something gets in your way. Get in the habit of praying all the time.

GOD IS OUR SAFE PLACE AND OUR STRENGTH.
HE IS ALWAYS OUR HELP WHEN WE ARE IN TROUBLE.
PSALM 46:1

FANNY CROSBY
{1820–1915}

The Girl with Nine Thousand Ideas

never undertake a hymn without first asking the good Lord to be my inspiration." And God, indeed, gave Fanny Crosby the inspiration she asked Him to provide. So much, in fact, that she wrote nearly nine thousand hymns—even though Fanny had been blind almost since birth!

Fanny didn't allow blindness to stop her from writing or doing anything else. At the New York Institute for the Blind, where Fanny stayed for twenty-three years, she not only learned to do what most sighted people can do, but she also taught other blind students.

Her poetry writing led Fanny to meet presidents, governors, and other famous people. She even read one of her poems in the United States Senate chamber in Washington, DC. Her poems were published in books, but none made Fanny famous until she began writing lyrics for hymns and Sunday school songs. Soon almost everyone knew her name.

Sometimes Fanny needed ideas for her lyrics. When she asked God for help, the ideas came!

Fanny praised God for her blindness. "If perfect earthly sight were offered me tomorrow, I would not accept it," she said. "I might not have sung hymns to the praise of God if I had been distracted by the beautiful and interesting things about me."

Maybe you need ideas sometimes for school projects or other things. Ask for God's help. You can trust that His ideas are good. After all, He created the earth and everything on it, He created the universe, and He created *you*!

EVERYTHING COMES FROM [GOD].
ROMANS 11:36

DOROTHY DAY
{1897–1980}

Helping the Poor

When I die, I hope people will say that I tried to be mindful of what Jesus told us—His wonderful stories—and I tried my best to live up to His example." Those words came from Dorothy Day.

Dorothy was born in 1897. As a young woman in the early 1900s, her career in journalism led Dorothy to New York, where she chose friends who lived in ways not always pleasing to God. Dorothy made many mistakes at that time in her life, but on the day she became a mom, Dorothy felt the need to be closer to God. When her friends saw her becoming more religious, many left her.

In her heart, Dorothy felt God leading her to help the poor. So she asked Him to show her how she might use her faith and writing skills to help others.

Several years later, Dorothy met a man named Peter Maurin. He shared with her ideas about helping the poor through what Jesus taught. Together they started a newspaper called *The Catholic Worker*. It encouraged readers to be like Jesus and serve others. Dorothy and Peter set up a soup kitchen and a "house of hospitality"—a place where poor people could find help. Before long, people volunteered to help, and more houses of hospitality were set up. The Catholic Worker movement, as it was called, grew bigger and bigger. It exists even today in two hundred Catholic Worker communities worldwide.

Dorothy Day spent the rest of her life serving the poor, and she always made time to pray. "The thing to remember," she said, "is not to read so much or talk so much about God, but to talk to God."

"THE POOR WILL ALWAYS BE IN THE LAND. SO I TELL YOU TO BE FREE IN GIVING TO YOUR BROTHER, TO THOSE IN NEED, AND TO THE POOR IN YOUR LAND."
DEUTERONOMY 15:11

Deborah
{JUDGES 4-5}

Judge Deborah

Close your eyes and imagine what a judge looks like. Did you picture someone sitting behind a desk and wearing a black robe? Deborah was a judge sometime around 1150 BC. She looked nothing like today's judges. She held court under a palm tree named for her. While she sat under the Deborah Tree, the Israelites brought her their disagreements.

Deborah was very wise. Like Anna, she was a prophetess. God spoke to her, and then she told others what He said.

She told a warrior named Barak that God wanted him and his troops to fight against an army led by a general named Sisera. His army was going after the Israelites, and God wanted the Israelites—His people—to be saved.

Barak agreed to go, but he insisted that Deborah go with him. So she did. And with them in charge of the troops, the Israelites won the battle. But that isn't where the story ends.

Today judges might close a case by pounding their gavel—a wooden hammer—one time on their desk or simply by saying, "Case closed." Deborah ended the case against Sisera's army in a different way. She prayed and praised God for the victory. She did it by singing.

Deborah's Song, her prayer, takes up all of chapter 5 in the book of Judges. Can you imagine a judge getting up and singing a thank-you prayer to God today?

Every day God gives you many little victories—little ways that you are successful—like doing well on a test, winning a game, or learning to do something new. Do you remember to thank Him? Get in the habit of ending each day by saying, or singing, a thank-you prayer.

. . . .

"O give thanks to the Lord. Call upon His name. Let the people know what He has done. Sing to Him. Sing praises to Him. Tell of all His great works."
1 Chronicles 16:8-9

SHIRLEY DOBSON
{C. 1936-}

Let's All Pray!

Pop quiz: What event happens in America every year on the first Thursday in May? If you guessed the National Day of Prayer, you're right! The first Thursday in May is a day set aside for people of all faiths to pray together for America.

For twenty-five years, Shirley Dobson led the organizing of the National Day of Prayer. Can you imagine what a huge job it was, encouraging all Americans to pray?

Shirley had been praying all her life. Her parents divorced when she was little. Her dad wasn't around much. Shirley saw her mother struggle to support her family. Each night, Shirley asked God to bring them a stepdad who would love and care for them. God answered that prayer with a *yes*. Shirley's mom met and married a good man named Joe, who became a wonderful father to Shirley. Years later when Shirley was a young woman, she prayed for a husband for herself. God said yes to that prayer too. Shirley married James Dobson, and together they dedicated their lives to serving God and built a huge ministry that focuses on families.

When Shirley was asked to lead the National Day of Prayer, at first she said no. She was already too busy. But God wanted her to do it. He kept speaking to her heart, telling her to say yes. When Shirley heard that some of her dearest friends also prayed for her to take the job, she agreed. Shirley got to work and helped grow the National Day of Prayer. Today millions of people make time on the first Thursday in May to pray for the United States, its leaders, and others.

Have you felt like Shirley and wanted to say no when God wanted you to say yes? Listen, and ask Him to show you His plan.

SHOW ME YOUR WAYS, O LORD. TEACH ME YOUR PATHS.
PSALM 25:4

ROMA DOWNEY
{1960-}

A Prayer-Centered Life

Prayer is important to actor and producer Roma Downey. She prays about every decision, big and small. When she works as an actress, she prays before she acts. In Roma's role as a producer, she prays for God's guidance.

Most of Roma's work in Hollywood is centered on her Christian faith. She played the role of the angel Monica in the television series *Touched by an Angel*. She produced the popular miniseries *The Bible* for the History Channel and the feature film *Son of God*. Roma has also written books for kids and adults. She is always thinking of the next great project through which she can share God's love with the world.

Roma grew up in an Irish family that loved God. Her parents taught her to pray. When Roma was just ten years old, her mom died. Roma's dad helped the family face the tragedy by putting their faith and trust in God. She remembers how comforted she felt sitting on her dad's knee while he read to her from the Bible. His love helped Roma to trust in God's unconditional love.

Prayer led Roma to her husband, Mark Burnett, creator of the hit television shows *The Voice*, *Are You Smarter Than a 5th Grader?*, *Shark Tank*, and others. You might say that theirs is a match made in heaven. Roma asked God to choose her husband, and when she saw Mark for the first time, in a hair salon, Roma knew he was the one. The couple got married, and today they enjoy praying and working together as they create new movies and television shows based on the truth of God's love. What's next from this Christian couple? Only time will tell, but it's sure to be something wonderful!

HEAR MY PRAYER, O GOD. LISTEN TO THE WORDS OF MY MOUTH.
PSALM 54:2

FAYE EDGERTON
{1889–1968}

What Language Does God Speak?

Have you ever wondered if God understands you when you pray? Does He speak your language? He does! God created every language on earth. He understands when you pray in English, when your Hispanic friend prays in Spanish, or when your friend in Uganda prays in Swahili. God is much smarter than humans, but He relies on humans to share His Word, the Bible, with others. That might be a problem if the Bible doesn't exist in someone's language.

Faye Edgerton, an American missionary, understood the importance of sharing the Bible with others. She served in Korea, learning the language and teaching the Bible to the Korean people. Teaching the people was easy because the Bible had been translated into their language. Then Faye was asked to return to America and serve a Navajo reservation in Arizona.

Faye did not speak Navajo, so she used an interpreter—someone who knew both English and Navajo—to speak to the people. When she tried to teach from the Bible, the translation often got messed up! Faye needed to learn their language so she could teach them the Bible. She asked her family to pray with her that God would help her learn one of the most difficult languages in the world.

God heard. And He helped Faye learn. He had even more for her to do. God led her to leave missionary work and become a Bible translator. Faye and two of her friends worked together to translate the New Testament, the story of Jesus and His followers, into Navajo. Today the New Testament exists not only in Navajo but also in more than fifteen hundred other languages.

Maybe you would like to learn another language so you can tell others about Jesus. If you pray, God will lead you.

THERE ARE MANY LANGUAGES IN THE WORLD. ALL OF THEM HAVE MEANING TO THE PEOPLE WHO UNDERSTAND THEM.
1 CORINTHIANS 14:10

ESTHER
{ESTHER 2:1-9:32}

"If I Die, I Die"

Esther, a Jewish orphan, lived with her cousin Mordecai in a time when their king was searching for a wife. The king wanted the kingdom's most beautiful woman, and he chose Esther! But then the story takes a twist. Mordecai told Esther, "Keep it a secret that you are a Jew." (The Bible doesn't explain why.)

Esther became queen. And when Mordecai hung around outside the palace to check on her, he overheard a plot to kill the king. Mordecai told Esther, and she told her husband. The king was so grateful that he wrote Mordecai's name in his remembrance book.

One of the king's men, Haman, hated Jews. When he saw Mordecai hanging around, he commanded him to bow. The king's subjects were supposed to bow to his men, but Mordecai refused. So, to get back at Mordecai, Haman made up lies about the Jews and convinced the king to have all the Jews killed.

Mordecai found out, and he told Esther. But Esther worried that if she told the king, she might die with the rest of the Jews. She needed to tell her husband and save her people. But what would happen then? Esther told Mordecai to have all the Jews pray for her, and she would pray too. Esther trusted in the power of prayer, and she gave her problem to God. "If I die, I die," she said.

When Esther revealed to the king that she was Jewish and asked him to save her people, he agreed. The king remembered Mordecai, the Jew who saved his life. And in the end, he punished Haman for his lies!

Read the rest of Esther's story in the Bible (Esther 1–10). And remember—when you ask God for help, don't worry. You can trust Him to solve your problems.

DO NOT WORRY. LEARN TO PRAY ABOUT EVERYTHING.
GIVE THANKS TO GOD AS YOU ASK HIM FOR WHAT YOU NEED.
PHILIPPIANS 4:6

ALLYSON FELIX
{1985-}

To Glorify Him

Olympic runner Allyson Felix is a winner! She has collected more Olympic gold medals than any other female track and field athlete. She works hard, trains hard, and runs hard. And when she wins, she gives all the credit to God! She knows her talent comes from Him, and whatever Allyson does, she does to honor Him. Allyson believes that giving glory to God is her purpose.

Allyson says that faith is the most important thing in her life. She grew up in a Christian home, the daughter of a pastor, and committed her life to Jesus when she was a little girl. Her parents taught her to read the Bible, memorize scripture, and pray.

Running fast is Allyson's talent, her gift from God. She is always striving to become better, but sometimes she messes up and doesn't win. Life is like that. Everyone messes up sometimes. When it happens to Allyson, she knows that God still loves her. She prays a lot and trusts Him to bring her peace whenever she is feeling stressed. "We always have our own idea of how our life is going to go, but we really have to follow the Lord's will," she says.

While continuing to train for the next Olympics, Allyson is concentrating on becoming smarter in the ways she trains and competes. Along with her running goals, Allyson has a more important lifelong goal: to become more like Jesus. Every day she prays to be more like Him so others might see what it is like to live with Jesus in their hearts.

Whatever your talent, Allyson Felix is your role model. Be like her. Pray all the time, work hard to do your best, and when you succeed, give all the glory to God.

· ·

LET US PUT EVERYTHING OUT OF OUR LIVES THAT KEEPS US FROM DOING WHAT WE SHOULD.
LET US KEEP RUNNING IN THE RACE THAT GOD HAS PLANNED FOR US.
HEBREWS 12:1

Margaret Fell
{1614–1702}

Mother of Quakerism

Margaret Fell lived in England at a time when kings ruled the church. There were many laws about how people could worship. Women were not allowed to serve the church or speak up about the government, church, and most other things.

When Margaret was sixteen, she married a wealthy judge, Thomas Fell. They lived in a mansion, Swarthmoor Hall, and Margaret quietly accepted the role of wife and, in time, mother to nine children. Twenty years passed, and then something life-changing happened.

A traveling preacher named George Fox visited Swarthmoor Hall. He had formed a new group of Christians called the Quakers. Their ideas differed from those of the king's church. Quakers believed people, both men and women, could speak directly to God. When Margaret listened to his ideas, she realized that women, like men, had the right to speak up about their beliefs and also serve in the church. She opened Swarthmoor Hall to others who believed in Quaker ideas, and it became their meeting place.

When she read the Bible, Margaret recognized that many women in its history had dared to speak up—so she would too! Margaret was put in prison for speaking up and not following rules set by the king's church. Still, that didn't stop her. She wrote about women's equality in the church, and her ideas were published.

After her husband, Thomas, died, Margaret married George Fox. Margaret became known as the Mother of Quakerism as she and George shared their Quaker ideas.

Her story teaches us that men and women are equal. God made us all. It shows us that everyone can speak directly with God in prayer. If Margaret were here, she might say, "Quiet yourself and listen for His voice."

Do you listen when you pray?

THE LORD SPOKE TO MOSES FACE TO FACE, AS A MAN SPEAKS TO HIS FRIEND.
EXODUS 33:11

KIM FIELDS
{1969–}

Celebrity!

It's difficult for celebrities to go most places because they are so easily recognized. This is true for Kim Fields. She became popular as a little girl when she starred in the television show *The Facts of Life*. More recently, Kim has been on *Dancing with the Stars* and other TV shows. When she wanted to visit the US Capitol, Kim and a small group of friends were offered a private, after-hours tour. When Kim saw all the amazing things inside, she said, "How are you not inspired to do great things in here?" Then she and her friends joined hands and prayed for the government leaders.

Faith is important to Kim. Her relationship with God began at age fourteen and brought her through the ups and downs that come with an acting career. In a business where it might be easy to get wrapped up in money and fame, Kim says her faith keeps her grounded.

Like everyone else, she has times when she feels sad, frustrated, or just plain overwhelmed by life! Kim has learned to be honest with God about her feelings. She finds time to stop, take a minute to pray, be still, and find peace.

At age forty-seven, Kim began to look back on her life and all the ways God had blessed her. Although she is very private about her personal life, Kim decided to write a book about her faith and the lessons she had learned about life. *Blessed Life: My Surprising Journey of Joy, Tears, and Tales from Harlem to Hollywood* was published in 2017.

Think about your life and all the ways God has blessed you. Then take a minute to thank Him for all He has done.

THANK GOD FOR HIS GREAT GIFT.
2 CORINTHIANS 9:15

Vonetta Flowers
{1973–}

Girl on a Sled

When she was nine years old, Vonetta Flowers dreamed of competing in the Olympics in track and field. She started with her elementary school track team. All the way through grade school and then in college, she won almost every event. Vonetta tried several times to earn a spot on the US Olympic track and field team, but something always got in the way—usually an injury. Finally, she decided God was trying to tell her something.

Vonetta had committed her life to Jesus after she met her future husband, Johnny Flowers, a Christian. Vonetta attended church with Johnny, and her faith grew strong. She prayed a lot, asking God to show her what to do next.

When Johnny saw a flyer encouraging track and field athletes to try out for the US bobsled team, something inside Vonetta said she should try. It was obvious she had talent. She made the team! Her job was giving the sled a running push at the beginning of the race. Vonetta was fast and able to give it a good start. After the push, she would jump in for the ride and then stop the sled with its brake at the end of the race.

In her very first race, Vonetta won an Olympic gold medal! She became the first African American to win gold in winter sports. When she won her medal, Vonetta understood everything had happened for a reason—God had led her toward realizing her dream but in a way she hadn't expected.

Vonetta relies on God and prayer to get her through every situation, and when she succeeds, she gives all the credit to Him. She believes it was prayer that helped her win the gold.

What are you praying for today?

I WILL SHOW YOU AND TEACH YOU IN THE WAY YOU SHOULD GO.
I WILL TELL YOU WHAT TO DO WITH MY EYE UPON YOU.
PSALM 32:8

ELIZABETH FRY
{1780-1845}

Angel to the Poor

Elizabeth Fry, a young girl growing up in England, didn't know what it was like to be poor. Her father was a banker, and he provided his children with more than they needed.

In her abundance, teenage Elizabeth became concerned about those who had very little. She even began to wonder if God existed. She wondered, *Why would God allow people to have so very little?* God heard her thoughts! And an idea was planted in her heart: rather than questioning God's existence, Elizabeth decided she should do something to help!

She began by collecting clothes for the poor and helping children who worked in factories. Elizabeth started a Sunday school for them and taught them to read, but she felt she wasn't doing nearly enough.

As an adult, she visited poor people in their homes. The conditions were bad! She did what she could to help, but Elizabeth still felt it wasn't enough. She needed a purpose—a specific goal.

And when Elizabeth visited a women's prison and saw the filthy, terrible place, she knew she had found her purpose. She became like an angel to the women there. She prayed for and with them, and she taught them to get along and be fair to one another. When the women wanted to set up a school in prison, Elizabeth helped make it happen.

Helping women in prison led Elizabeth into a lifetime of making things better for the poor. She became well known, and because of that, Elizabeth was able to get help from the queen and other leaders. Her mission grew throughout Europe. Prison life improved. Many people were helped by Elizabeth's kindness. She never gave up. She prayed hard and stood up to those who were against her, and she persisted until she got things done.

How can you be like Elizabeth and help others? Ask God to show you.

THE SPIRIT OF THE LORD GOD IS ON ME, BECAUSE THE LORD HAS CHOSEN ME TO BRING GOOD NEWS TO POOR PEOPLE. HE HAS SENT ME TO HEAL THOSE WITH A SAD HEART.

ISAIAH 61:1

KaTHIE LEE GIFFOrD
{1953-}

Sharing the Good News

Do you find it easy sharing your Christian faith with nonbelieving friends? Some Christians have a difficult time talking about Jesus, but Kathie Lee Gifford is not one of them! She talks about Jesus to anyone who will listen. She doesn't worry if they believe in Him or not. Kathie knows that she has a responsibility to share the Good News that Jesus is the only way to get to heaven. Whenever someone commits his or her life to Jesus as Savior and Lord, it makes Kathie happy.

As a famous singer and television personality, Kathie gets to meet and talk with many people. Whenever she can, she brings her Christian faith into her conversations. She likes to remind others of the power of prayer. The Bible says we should pray without stopping. Kathie Lee explains it this way: "Make your whole life a prayer." If you are thinking about God all the time and praying to Him all day, that helps your faith grow. God becomes part of everything you do, and you rely on Him not only for help with the big stuff but with the little stuff too.

Kathie's faith has led her through life. She committed her life to Jesus when she was twelve years old, and she considers Him her best Friend. Her trust in Him has helped Kathie know when someone is being real or phony, and that has kept her on track with living life as a Christian. One thing people notice about Kathie is that she is not afraid to speak up about her faith. In her role as a television talk show host, she often speaks about faith and prayer, reaching millions of viewers.

Be bold like Kathie Lee. Share your faith with others starting today.

I am not ashamed of the Good News. It is the Power of God. It is the way He saves men from the punishment of their sins if they put their trust in Him.
ROMANS 1:16

Morrow Graham
{1892–1981}

Billy's Mom

In a Christian home, praying is important and so is reading the Bible. Moms and dads make sure their kids grow up knowing about God and understanding what it means to live in ways pleasing to Him.

Maybe you have heard about Billy Graham. He was a famous preacher who led many people to the Lord, and he grew up in a Christian home. Billy's mother, Morrow Graham, was a mom who made sure her kids knew about Jesus. She and her husband gathered the whole family together every day to pray and listen to stories they read from the Bible. She made sure there were always good, Bible-based books lying around the house for her kids to read.

Morrow Graham prayed for her children all the time. Billy told others that when he was in school studying to be a preacher, his mom and dad knelt in their home every morning at ten o'clock and prayed for him. He was sure his mother's prayers were one of the reasons he found so much success as a preacher.

This was a time long before computers and smartphones. Long-distance communicating was done with letters. Morrow Graham often wrote to her son when he was in Bible school. On the day Billy Graham went away to school, she asked God to help her write letters that would encourage and help him. One of Billy's letters to his mom said he especially appreciated the cheerful letters she wrote to him. God had answered Mrs. Graham's prayer!

Praying together and for each other was important to Morrow Graham. Is it important to you? If you don't already share prayer time as a family, suggest that everyone get together to listen to Bible stories and pray.

"For where two or three are gathered together in my name,
there I am with them."
Matthew 18:20

RUTH BELL GRAHAM
{1920–2007}

Mr. Right

As a young woman, Ruth Bell wrote a prayer poem telling God about the kind of man she would like to marry. She told God her future husband didn't have to be handsome as long as he was doing his best to be like God. He didn't have to be big, strong, smart, or rich, but whoever he was, he needed to hold his head high as a child of God. She wanted a man who honored God with his whole life. And she wanted him to have "quiet eyes." Her prayer included plenty of details. When God sent her His Mr. Right, Ruth wanted to be sure to recognize him as God's answer to her prayer.

Ruth had dreamed of becoming a missionary in Tibet. But then she met a young preacher named Billy Graham. The two fell head-over-heels in love. Billy had two questions for Ruth. First, "Will you marry me?" Then, "Will you give up your dream of being a missionary and help me grow my ministry?" He felt in his heart that it was the right thing for her to do.

Giving up her dream to go to China wasn't an easy decision. Ruth prayed hard about it, and God put it in Ruth's heart that Billy was the Mr. Right she had asked for in her prayer poem.

So Ruth married Billy. They became the perfect team. Where he was weak, she was strong. Together they reached many more for Christ than Ruth would have if she had gone alone to Tibet.

Would you like to get married one day? Think about the kind of man you would like to marry. Start praying now and ask God to send you His Mr. Right.

THEN THE LORD GOD SAID, "IT IS NOT GOOD FOR MAN TO BE ALONE.
I WILL MAKE A HELPER THAT IS RIGHT FOR HIM."
GENESIS 2:18

AMY GRANT
{1960–}

Singer and Songwriter

Do you ever sing praise and worship songs and really focus on the words? If you think about it, it might seem as though the songs are really prayers. . . things you'd say to God when you're having a heart-to-heart conversation with Him. If you'd ask Amy Grant, she'd agree.

Amy started writing songs when she was fifteen. Her friends noticed how good her songs were and how great she sounded singing them. When Amy sang to a youth group at her church, one of the kids said that if she would allow God to be in charge of her talent, He would use her. Amy asked the kids to pray for her. She specifically asked them to pray that she wouldn't get in the way of the plans God had for her.

When she began singing with a purpose, to share the love of God with others, Amy became famous for introducing Christian songs into a pop music style. Her songs have won numerous awards, among them six Grammys.

Today, along with singing, Amy is a praying wife and mom. She doesn't have a set time and place for prayer. She just prays! She prays for a clean heart and a loving home, and for her relationship with her husband and for each of her kids. When she sees something awesome that God made, she thanks Him. She also considers her singing a form of prayer.

Amy says the most important thing she has learned about prayer is how deep God's love is for us. Amy has messed up sometimes in her life, but she knows that God always forgives her. When she asks for forgiveness, nothing separates her from Him. He is always ready to heal her guilt and forgive.

"COME NOW, LET US THINK ABOUT THIS TOGETHER," SAYS THE LORD. "EVEN THOUGH YOUR SINS ARE BRIGHT RED, THEY WILL BE AS WHITE AS SNOW. EVEN THOUGH THEY ARE DARK RED, THEY WILL BE LIKE WOOL."
ISAIAH 1:18

Fannie Lou Hamer
{1917-77}

Civil Rights Leader

Fannie Lou Hamer faced many obstacles in her lifetime. She grew up in the South a few decades after slavery ended. Her family was very poor with barely enough to live on. Issues facing African Americans became important to Fannie. She saw black people fighting for their rights, and when she was old enough, she joined in.

Church was where Fannie felt most welcome. After hearing a sermon there, she felt God leading black Americans to stand up for their rights, especially the right to vote.

Fannie and others traveled in an old beat-up bus to the courthouse where voter registration happened. Inside they were given a test. Fannie believed the questions were created to cause African Americans to fail. On the ride home, a police officer stopped the bus. He arrested the driver for operating a bus that was too yellow, too much like a school bus! That's when Fannie stood up and sang, encouraging everyone to pray and tell Jesus about their troubles.

Fannie spent the rest of her life leading the fight for equal rights. Singing to God and praying guided her beyond each obstacle in her way. In 1964, speaking to a committee of Democrats about the troubles African Americans faced, Fannie said, "I'm sick and tired of being sick and tired!"

Today Fannie is remembered as a hardworking leader in the civil rights movement, a woman unafraid of speaking her mind—*and* a woman who prayed.

"COME TO ME, ALL OF YOU WHO WORK AND HAVE HEAVY LOADS.
I WILL GIVE YOU REST."
MATTHEW 11:28

BETHANY HAMILTON-DIRKS
{1990-}

Surfer Girl

Bethany Hamilton and her mom enjoyed reading the Bible and praying together. One of their favorite scripture verses was Jeremiah 29:11: "'For I know the plans I have for you,' says the Lord, 'plans for well-being and not for trouble, to give you a future and a hope.'" Bethany trusted those words. She felt peace knowing that God had a plan for her.

On October 31, 2003, when Bethany was thirteen, her life changed forever. Bethany was an excellent surfer, often surfing in competitions. But that morning she surfed with her dad just for fun. She lay on her board, arms dangling in the water, waiting for a wave. Then, suddenly, Bethany felt pressure on her left arm. A hard pull joggled her arm a few times, and the water around her turned red. Bethany saw her left arm was missing at the shoulder. She managed to tell her dad, "I got attacked by a shark!" Then she asked God to rescue her.

Help arrived fast. In the ambulance on the way to the hospital, she remembers a paramedic saying, "God will never leave you nor forsake you." Bethany held on to those words. She knew God had rescued her.

The loss of her arm didn't keep Bethany from surfing. One month after the attack, she was back on her surfboard and winning more competitions. She became a pro surfer.

Today Bethany is a pastor's wife and a mom. She continues to surf and inspires others by giving speeches about surfing, the shark attack, and God. She believes that she is living God's plan for her life.

The next time you face trouble, think of Bethany Hamilton and remember that God is with you. Do what she did: ask for God's help.

"BE STRONG AND HAVE STRENGTH OF HEART! DO NOT BE AFRAID OR LOSE FAITH. FOR THE LORD YOUR GOD IS WITH YOU ANYWHERE YOU GO."
JOSHUA 1:9

HaNNaH
{1 SaMuel 1; 2:1–21}

An Unselfish Act

Hannah's story is about unselfishness. She wanted something. *Really* wanted it. But how far would she go to get it?

Hannah wanted a baby, a son. Her husband's other wife, Peninnah, had children. But Hannah had none. (Back then, men often had more than one wife.)

Peninnah made fun of Hannah because she had no children. The bullying made Hannah sad. But instead of feeling sorry for herself, she did something better. She went to the temple and prayed to God. Hannah told God how much she wanted a son. Then she did something amazingly unselfish. She promised God that if He gave her a son, she would share the boy with Him. Hannah promised to allow the temple priests to raise her son so he would grow up learning to serve His heavenly Father.

As Hannah knelt in the temple, crying and praying, the high priest Eli saw her. He asked about her troubles. Then Eli joined Hannah in prayer. They both asked God to bless Hannah with a son.

Some months later, baby Samuel was born! God gave Hannah what she wanted. And Hannah kept her promise to God. She allowed the temple priests to raise her little boy.

Samuel grew up to be a great man. He became a priest, a judge, and a prophet, and he is remembered even today for his wisdom.

Hannah wasn't sure God would give her a son. But when she prayed, she was willing to give her whole heart to God. She promised Him that if He blessed her, she would show her gratitude by giving Him control over her most precious possession, her son.

Could you be that unselfish?

· ·

"YOU MUST GIVE YOUR WHOLE HEART TO HIM AND HOLD
OUT YOUR HANDS TO HIM FOR HELP."
JOB 11:13 NCV

HILDEGARD OF BINGEN
{1098-1179}

Write It Down

Hildegard of Bingen was born in Germany during the Middle Ages—the time between the fall of the Roman Empire and the Renaissance. The only recognized religion was Christianity, and the only church in Europe was the Catholic Church. When she was eight years old, Hildegard's parents sent her to live with a Catholic woman named Jutta who could provide Hildegard with a religious education. Hildegard learned how to write, read the Psalms, and chant prayers to God. Later, as a young woman, she became a nun and led a Benedictine convent.

Throughout her life, Hildegard had visions of light in which she saw things. She didn't understand what they meant. Then, at age forty-two, she envisioned a fiery, flashing light from heaven. It poured into her, warming her heart. Hildegard knew then that God wanted her to be a prophet—one who speaks His words to others. She began writing about her visions. "I spoke and wrote these things not by the invention of my heart or that of any other person," she said, "but as by the secret mysteries of God; I heard and received them in the heavenly places. And again I heard a voice from heaven saying to me, 'Cry out therefore, and write thus!'"

Hildegard wrote not only about what God told her when she talked with Him in prayer. She also wrote about science and medicine. She wrote plays and music. She even traveled around Germany, preaching what she had learned from God.

Along with the importance of listening to God in prayer, Hildegard's story teaches the value of keeping a prayer journal. If you sense God telling you something, write it down. Then you can keep track of what you pray for and how God answers your prayers.

. . . .

"WRITE DOWN THE VISION. . .SO WHOEVER READS IT CAN RUN TO TELL OTHERS."
HABAKKUK 2:2 NCV

FAITH HILL
{1967-}

It Began with a Prayer

Did you know that country singer Faith Hill was an adopted child? Her adoption began with a prayer. Faith's parents, Ted and Edna Perry, had two boys. They wanted to adopt a girl. So they asked God to send them a baby. When their prayers went unanswered, they talked with a doctor friend. They asked if he would tell them if he were to hear of a woman who wanted to place her baby daughter for adoption. Faith's parents wondered if anything would come of it, but within a week they received a call. A young woman had just given birth to a baby girl. The woman wanted her baby to have a better life than she could provide. The Perrys praised God! They named their adopted baby Audrey Faith. Her middle name was her parents' way of thanking God for His faithfulness in answering their prayer.

The Perrys were Christian, and Faith grew up trusting Jesus. It was obvious to the Perrys that Faith had a God-given talent to sing. She began singing at age three! When she was seven, Faith attended an Elvis Presley concert. Elvis was known as "the king of rock and roll," and when Faith heard him perform, she was sure she wanted a singing career. When she became a teen, Faith learned to play the guitar, and she started her own country music band.

Faith moved to Nashville, hoping to cut an album. She relied on prayer, and before long she was recording records. Her first single became a number-one hit!

Today Faith is famous. She is one of the most well-known country singers in the world. She and her husband, country singer Tim McGraw, are both Christians. They pray together and center their lives on Jesus.

"I PRAYED FOR THIS CHILD, AND THE LORD HAS GRANTED ME WHAT I ASKED OF HIM."
1 SAMUEL 1:27 NIV

ANNE HUTCHINSON
{1591-1643}

The Courage to Speak Up

Anne Hutchinson was raised by parents who taught her to always think for herself and question others' beliefs—even if it wasn't the popular thing to do. She grew up during a time in England's history when the Church of England decided what people should do and say—it was the law! But Anne's dad disagreed with their teaching, and he taught Anne to question their rules too—especially when it came to religion.

When Anne was older, she married William Hutchinson. Both disliked the Church of England, so they moved across the ocean to the Massachusetts Bay Colony in America. There they expected to have complete freedom to believe and worship as they pleased. But that isn't what happened. The colony's governor, John Winthrop, wanted everyone to follow strict Puritan rules, which included that women were to keep their beliefs quiet while men took the lead.

But Anne, who thought for herself, decided she wasn't going to keep quiet! She led prayer meetings in her house where people could pray together and discuss religion. In time the number of people attending her meetings grew. Many began questioning the beliefs of the Puritan Church of Boston, and that upset Governor Winthrop—a lot!

Winthrop said that Anne's prayer meetings were not legal, so he put Anne on trial for heresy—teaching something that was against what the church believed. At her trial, Anne challenged the beliefs of the Boston church. She answered the governor's questions by quoting Bible verses. Winthrop thought Anne's answers were very disrespectful, and she was kicked out of the colony!

Anne Hutchinson bravely prayed in public and shared her faith with others. She was one of the first American women to speak up about her faith. Her actions helped give more women the courage to continue speaking up and fighting for what they believe.

"BE STRONG AND HAVE STRENGTH OF HEART. DO NOT BE AFRAID OR SHAKE WITH FEAR. . . .
FOR THE LORD YOUR GOD IS THE ONE WHO GOES WITH YOU."
DEUTERONOMY 31:6

ESTHER IBANGA
{1961-}

Praying for Peace

In Nigeria, where Esther Ibanga is a pastor, Christians and Muslims don't get along. They are at war with one another, and there is no peace. Esther felt the pain of war among the people when her mother's home was set on fire. Anger rose up inside Esther. She prayed to God, telling Him about her angry feelings. She wanted nothing to do with Muslims.

Then, when Christian women in her community came to her saying, "Pastor, we can't let this go on. What can we do?" Esther decided not to allow anger to take hold. She did something almost unheard of. She reached out to Muslim women, hoping that together they might find a solution. She discovered Muslims faced the same anger when Christian young people burned their homes. The idea that they had things in common led Esther to forgive.

She and her new friends began the Women Without Walls Initiative. Their goal is to reach the children of Nigeria and help them learn to get along so someday there might be peace.

Her work is sometimes criticized by Christians in Nigeria who want nothing to do with Muslims. Still, Esther sees lives being changed through Women Without Walls. She believes the only way to bring peace is through Jesus and His teachings on hope and love. She says, "God is ready to transform lives if we let Him use us."

Esther was raised in a family that prayed. "We were born and raised into an atmosphere of prayer," she said. Today Esther prays for peace among Christians, Muslims, and all people everywhere in the world.

Do you pray for peace in the world? Think of three things you can do to help people get along.

"DO NOT HURT SOMEONE WHO HAS HURT YOU. DO NOT KEEP ON HATING THE SONS OF YOUR PEOPLE, BUT LOVE YOUR NEIGHBOR AS YOURSELF."
LEVITICUS 19:18

Immaculée Ilibagiza
{1972-}

"I Forgive You"

Immaculée Ilibagiza's story isn't pretty, but she tells it anyway. She tells it to teach others that the cure for fear is praying and trusting God. She inspires others to find peace even when anger fills their hearts.

Immaculée had grown up in a village in Rwanda, Africa. She was attending college and was home on Easter break when war broke out between two tribes, the Hutus and the Tutsis. The Hutus began killing Tutsis as revenge for the assassination of the Hutu president. No one was spared. The Hutus murdered men, women, and children.

Immaculée's family belonged to the Tutsi tribe. To protect Immaculée, her dad told her to run to a pastor's house, where she could hide. The kind Hutu pastor sheltered Immaculée and seven other women in his tiny bathroom. From there, Immaculée could imagine all the terrible things happening outside.

For ninety-one days, eight women stayed in that tiny room. Immaculée prayed they wouldn't be discovered. Praying and reading a Bible she brought with her helped to bring Immaculée peace. But anger boiled inside her too. The Bible said to forgive those who hurt her, but Immaculée wasn't sure she could—not until she remembered Jesus' prayer as He hung on the cross: "Father, forgive them; for they know not what they do" (Luke 23:34 KJV). All at once, Immaculée felt a certain peace—even joy—at the thought of forgiving.

When it was safe for Immaculée to come out of hiding, she discovered her entire family, except one brother, had been murdered. She knew the only way to find peace was to forgive. So Immaculée visited her family's killer in prison, and she told him sincerely, "I forgive you."

Has someone caused you to feel hurt or angry? Remember Immaculée's story. Ask God to give you courage to forgive.

"Forgive us our sins as we forgive those who sin against us."
Matthew 6:12

Kathy Ireland
{1963–}

Super Role Model

When Kathy Ireland committed her life to Jesus, something inside her changed. She realized that self-esteem, confidence in one's own worth, doesn't come as a result of good looks. Or wealth. Or how smart someone is. Confidence in self-worth comes from knowing how deeply Jesus loves you.

Kathy became a Christian at age eighteen. She had just arrived in Paris, France, to begin a modeling career. When she opened her suitcase in her room, Kathy found a Bible that her mother had packed. Kathy had never read the Bible, but there was nothing else in the room to read, and she was bored. She opened it up and began reading the book of Matthew. As she read about Jesus, Kathy discovered He was nothing like she had imagined. He was loving and compassionate. A leader. She thought Jesus was cool, so she made Him her best Friend.

Her modeling career skyrocketed! Kathy became a supermodel, business-woman, wife, and mom. Jesus remained a part of her life, but He didn't come first. She was trying to mold Jesus into what she wanted Him to be instead of allowing Him to make her into what He wanted *her* to be. Kathy was praying one day when Jesus spoke to her heart. He said she needed to make Him her first priority. "I don't know how," she said. Jesus answered, "Trust Me."

Kathy began spending more time with Jesus, praying and forming a deeper relationship with Him. By putting Him first, Kathy quickly understood what a perfect leader Jesus is for her and her family. Today she makes Jesus her first priority in everything. She chooses to follow Him, believing He knows the right way to go.

Think about it. Is Jesus *your* first priority?

· ·

JESUS SAID TO HIM, " 'YOU MUST LOVE THE LORD YOUR GOD WITH ALL YOUR HEART AND WITH ALL YOUR SOUL AND WITH ALL YOUR MIND.' "
MATTHEW 22:37

Mahalia Jackson
{1911-72}

World-Famous Gospel Singer

When twelve-year-old Mahalia Jackson sang in church, her beautiful, strong voice carried all the way outside. "You going to be famous in this world and walk with kings and queens," Mahalia's aunt Bell said. And she was right!

Mahalia began singing professionally in her late teens. She loved singing gospel music. Its lyrics were full of emotion. The beat was bouncy and strong like the blues, but different. Mahalia wanted nothing to do with secular music—music with lyrics that weren't Christian. It would have been easy for her to find work as a blues singer, but Mahalia made a promise to God that she would use her voice only to honor Him.

A famous African American composer and piano player, Thomas Dorsey, heard Mahalia sing. Dorsey had been actively working to bring gospel music into the mainstream. He invited Mahalia to go on tour with him. This led to many people hearing her sing, and before long she became famous.

Mahalia made records, and she even had her own radio show. Soon she was appearing as a guest on television variety shows and performing not only in America but also in Europe. Using her voice to honor God had led Mahalia to becoming an international star.

"Faith and prayer are the vitamins of the soul," Mahalia said. She often sang about faith and praying. Her own faith and prayers led her to win three Grammy Awards for best gospel recording. Even more important, she was honored to sing at President John F. Kennedy's inaugural ball and was invited by Dr. Martin Luther King Jr. to sing at the March on Washington for civil rights in the 1960s.

Mahalia Jackson is remembered today as one of the greatest gospel singers ever, a result of her keeping her promise to God.

Have you made a promise to God? If so, ask Him to help you keep it!

My lips will shout for joy when I sing praise to you—I whom you have delivered.
Psalm 71:23 niv

JOCHEBED
{EXODUS 1; 2:1-10}

A Mother's Faith

The Bible doesn't say Jochebed prayed, but you can imagine she did, or at least tried. You'll understand why when you read her story:

Egypt's king, Pharaoh, hated Jews. Their men were becoming too many and too powerful. So Pharaoh ordered his people to drown all the Jewish baby boys.

Jochebed had a newborn son, and no way would she let him die! For three months, she hid him. But as he grew bigger, hiding him became difficult. Jochebed needed to let him go and trust that somehow God would save him. She put her baby into a basket and set it in tall grass by the Nile River where women went to bathe. Then she told her daughter, Miriam, to hide and watch.

What happened next might have been awful, but God worked it out for good. The king's daughter found the baby! She could have told her dad, but instead she decided to save the Jewish boy. She saw Miriam nearby. "Go! Find a Jewish nurse to care for the baby until I can find a way to keep him," she said.

Who did Miriam bring back? Jochebed!

God allowed Jochebed to care for her baby a little while longer, until the king's daughter wanted him back. It was hard for Jochebed to let him go, but she knew he would be safe in the king's palace.

That little boy grew up to be Moses, one of the Jews' greatest heroes.

God knows what you need before you ask Him. The Bible is filled with stories like Jochebed's to prove it. Sometimes it might be hard for you to pray. If that happens, it's enough to know that God is always with you. When trouble comes, He will lead you through it.

WE KNOW THAT GOD MAKES ALL THINGS WORK TOGETHER FOR THE GOOD OF
THOSE WHO LOVE HIM AND ARE CHOSEN TO BE A PART OF HIS PLAN.
ROMANS 8:28

SHAWN JOHNSON
{1992-}

Gymnast

When Shawn Johnson was three years old, her mom enrolled her in a gymnastics class. Shawn loved it! A few years later, she began training with an instructor who recognized Shawn was good enough to make America's gymnastic Olympics team. She needed to be sixteen to compete, so Shawn had plenty of years to work at becoming the best at floor exercise and the balance beam.

Finally, she was old enough. In 2008 Shawn went to the Summer Olympics in Beijing, China. She won four medals, one gold and three silvers. But Shawn wasn't happy. Those silver medals made her feel like she wasn't good enough. She had given 200 percent and still, she thought, had failed the world.

Everyone knew her name, and being famous was hard for Shawn. In 2012 as she trained for the next Olympics, Shawn was totally stressed out. She felt she needed to be perfect to please her coach, the team, her sponsors, and everyone else. Then, one day, she was training on the balance beam when something unusual occurred. Shawn says it happened in an instant. God spoke to her heart and said, "You've been so distraught over this decision. . . . You've been afraid of disappointing a lot of people. . . . It's okay to follow your heart." Shawn felt the weight of the world lift off her shoulders. She had been taught by her parents to talk with God, and now He was talking to her!

From Shawn's courageous story, we can see that she came to understand that winning and being perfect didn't matter. The only thing that did matter was God. She discovered He is the answer to everything.

Shawn followed her heart and retired from competition. Today she is married, has a successful YouTube channel, and does charity work.

"YOU WILL KNOW THE TRUTH AND THE TRUTH WILL MAKE YOU FREE."
JOHN 8:32

Tamara Jolee {Metcalfe}
{1980-}

"Lord, What's Next?"

Tamara Jolee is an award-winning reporter. Her job is telling true stories about every imaginable topic. Along with reporting the news, she had her own television show featuring sports. She has told stories about when she traveled to Malawi, Africa, to serve "God's children" there. Tamara has lived in eight states and on three continents, reporting news from around the world. But her most important story isn't about any of these things. The story she tells most often now is about how God is helping her live with a life-threatening illness.

Tamara has cancer, a blood cancer that might take her life. She is fighting it and winning so far, but she knows most people with her kind of cancer live only about five to seven years.

Everything had been going so well for her career when Tamara received the news that she had cancer. She could have asked God, "Why me?" Instead, she prayed, "Lord, what's next?" When she prayed, Tamara felt peace. God was telling her that whatever happened, it would be okay.

Even before cancer, Tamara knew that her personal relationship with Jesus meant everything. She had asked Jesus to come into her heart and had learned to surrender her life to Him. She learned to live in the moment rather than worrying about what comes next. Tamara trusts Jesus to lead her, and she is at peace knowing that He is on her side.

Tamara Jolee's story reminds us that even in the worst of times, Jesus is with us. He brings us peace. Today, while Tamara continues to work as a reporter, Jesus is using her illness to encourage not only people fighting cancer but also everyone who needs Him to come into their lives.

. . . .

THE PEACE OF GOD IS MUCH GREATER THAN THE HUMAN MIND CAN UNDERSTAND.
THIS PEACE WILL KEEP YOUR HEARTS AND MINDS THROUGH CHRIST JESUS.
PHILIPPIANS 4:7

Mary Jones
{1784–1864}

Mary's Long Walk

Mary Jones lived in a stone cottage in the Welsh countryside. Green grass was everywhere. In the distance she could see the sea. It all looked very pleasant. But Mary Jones and her mother were poor. They worked hard to get by.

There were no cars then, and people traveled mostly in carts pulled by animals or by walking. Every Sunday Mary and her mom walked a mile and a half to attend church. Mary loved hearing Bible stories. She prayed, asking God to help her learn to read so she could read the Bible herself. Then, when she could read, Mary decided she wanted a Bible of her own.

They were too poor to buy a Bible, so Mary decided to do little jobs for people and save the money she earned. For six years she saved until she had enough for a Bible. But when she went to buy one, there were none for sale in her village. The nearest place where she could get one was twenty-six miles away.

Mary took a walk—a *very long* walk! When she arrived at the home of the Reverend Thomas Charles, the place where she could buy a Bible, he had just one left. It was promised to someone else. When the reverend realized how far Mary had walked, he gave her the Bible.

Mary's story doesn't end there. Reverend Charles wanted everyone to have a Bible, so he started a Bible society, a group willing to translate the Bible into many different languages and distribute it around the world. His Bible society exists to this day, thanks to a little girl named Mary Jones.

How far would you be willing to walk to buy a Bible?

YOUR WORD IS A LAMP TO MY FEET AND A LIGHT TO MY PATH.
PSALM 119:105

ANN HASSELTINE JUDSON
{1789-1826}

First Woman Missionary Overseas

Ann Hasseltine was a teenager when she committed her life to Jesus. And when she was just seventeen years old, she began teaching school. Her primary goal was to see her pupils commit their lives to Jesus too. In her diary, Ann wrote about how she began each school day with a prayer. She also wrote about how she wanted to see nations who had never heard of Jesus come to know Him. If you read the words in Ann's diary, it would be no surprise that God was preparing Ann to become a missionary.

Ann spent time talking to God and studying the Bible. She asked God where He wanted her to go, and God heard. Ann would become the first woman missionary overseas!

She met a young minister, Adoniram Judson, who shared the dream of becoming an overseas missionary. The couple fell in love, got married, and sailed to India—where they soon discovered they weren't welcome! So, instead, they traveled to Burma (modern Myanmar), a country between India and China. The people of Burma hadn't heard about Jesus. And Ann and Adoniram were exactly where God wanted them.

Ann and her husband had a difficult time explaining the good news of Jesus in the Burmese language. But Ann was determined to figure it out. She translated the Gospel so the people could understand, and they began surrendering their lives to Jesus.

Ann also wrote about her missionary work, and her stories influenced many women to become missionaries in faraway lands too, which was the best part of God's plan. Because He sent Ann, it's now common for American women to serve as missionaries overseas.

Just as He did for Ann Judson, God has a plan for everyone—including *you*! If you are willing to follow Jesus wherever He wants you to go, ask Him to use you.

THEN JESUS SAID TO THEM ALL, "IF ANYONE WANTS TO FOLLOW ME, HE MUST GIVE UP HIMSELF AND HIS OWN DESIRES. HE MUST TAKE UP HIS CROSS EVERYDAY AND FOLLOW ME."
LUKE 9:23

JULIAN OF NORWICH
{1342–1416}

What Julian Saw

Julian of Norwich was the first woman to write a book in English. Her book *Revelations of Divine Love* is read even today, many centuries after she wrote it.

Not much is known about Julian except what she prayed for and what happened next. She wanted a deeper understanding of God, so Julian prayed a daring prayer. She prayed that while she was still young, God would allow her to become sick with a life-threatening illness! But there was more. She asked Him not to let her die, but rather to allow her to experience what a soul might see in death. In other words, she prayed for a near-death experience.

God answered, giving Julian what she asked for. At age thirty, she suffered a life-threatening disease. Julian claimed she saw sixteen visions of Jesus and heaven during the time she was ill. When she became well again, she wrote them down.

Julian wrote that she had seen Jesus' crown of thorns and what His face looked like when others were cruel to Him. She discovered that God is in all things, and nothing happens by chance. Julian saw that Jesus washes away our sins and that sin is overcome because of His death. And God showed Julian that there is joy in heaven. He keeps us safe in good times and bad. She understood there was no greater pain than what Jesus suffered, but He suffered it for us. Then she saw Jesus' loving heart and His mother, Mary. Julian felt God's greatness and how important it is to pray. She recognized that heaven is amazing and that Jesus is truly there.

Could you imagine praying such a prayer and receiving such an answer? Today people read Julian's book hoping for a little glimpse of heaven.

LET US HONOR AND THANK THE GOD AND FATHER OF OUR LORD JESUS CHRIST.
HE HAS ALREADY GIVEN US A TASTE OF WHAT HEAVEN IS LIKE.
EPHESIANS 1:3

HeLeN KeLLer
{1880-1968}

The Power to Do More

If you have sight, you know what things look like. But what if you were like Helen Keller and could not see or hear? Close your eyes and cover your ears to shut out any sound. What's it like inside you when you are alone in there with your thoughts?

Helen Keller was made blind and deaf by an illness when she was a little girl. For a while, it seemed impossible that she could learn anything or make much out of her life. But then a teacher, Anne Sullivan, helped Helen to learn and live in the unseen world around her.

In her inside world, Helen was not alone. God was with her. She could sense His love, learn from His wisdom, and feel His power working through her. She could imagine what she could not see and assign it beauty all its own. By reading her Braille Bible, Helen could dig out facts, truths about God that she could apply to her own life.

About prayer, Helen said, "It is for us to pray not for tasks equal to our powers, but for powers equal to our tasks." In other words, she said we should pray not to do only what we can but pray for the power to do even more. With God's help, Helen accomplished more. She learned to read, write, and speak. She graduated from college and toured the world, giving speeches and meeting famous people. She became known around the world and received many awards. Helen even married.

Maybe you have a disability, like Helen, or maybe there is something you want to do even better. Don't let it get you down. Remember Helen's story. Ask God to give you power to do more.

I CAN DO ALL THINGS BECAUSE CHRIST GIVES ME THE STRENGTH.
PHILIPPIANS 4:13

CORETTA SCOTT KING
{1927-2006}

Strength, Hope, and Prayer

Coretta Scott King, wife of civil rights leader Dr. Martin Luther King Jr., was a praying woman committed to her husband's dream of people of all colors living equally and in peace.

Throughout their struggle for freedom, Coretta King's hope grew through the power of prayer. When hatred resulted in African Americans' homes being burned and bombed, when black people were killed because of the color of their skin, prayer brought Coretta hope. She had faith that with God's grace the suffering would eventually lead to something good.

Prayer was a regular part of Mrs. King's life, and her husband's as well. On one difficult night after someone had threatened the lives of Dr. King and his family, Mrs. King heard her husband pray. He told God he felt what he was doing was right, but he couldn't do it alone. After he prayed, Dr. King said he felt Christ's presence in the most powerful way. It left him with a new sense of confidence. Coretta viewed his prayer as a turning point in the civil rights movement.

Coretta Scott King believed prayer provides strength and hope when we face obstacles. When we open our hearts to God in prayer, we open ourselves to His perfect will. She demonstrated this as she faced the worst obstacle of her life. Strength and hope led Mrs. King to go to Memphis just four days after her husband had been murdered there. "I believe that this nation can be transformed into a society of love and justice, peace and brotherhood where all men can really be brothers," she said.

When you pray today, pray for your nation and its leaders. Pray for peace and acceptance for everyone.

HAPPY IS THE NATION WHOSE GOD IS THE LORD.
HAPPY ARE THE PEOPLE HE HAS CHOSEN FOR HIS OWN.
PSALM 33:12

Jarena Lee
{1783–1849}

"Go Preach the Gospel"

Today it's not unusual to see pastors of every nationality, both men and women. But in Jarena Lee's time, most pastors were white men. Can you imagine Jarena's surprise when she, an African American woman, heard God's voice tell her, "Go preach the Gospel"?

"No one will believe me!" Jarena answered. She waited to hear if God would reply.

He did. "Preach the Gospel," God said. "I will put words in your mouth and will turn your enemies to become your friends."

Jarena went to her African American church and asked Pastor Richard Allen, a former slave, if she could preach. At first he felt uncomfortable allowing it. Not because Jarena was black, but because she was a woman. Finally, Pastor Allen agreed that God had called Jarena to preach the Gospel. She became the first African American woman to preach publicly.

She had little education, but Jarena became a self-taught traveling preacher. She lived in a time when slavery was legal and white people owned slaves. Still, she traveled around preaching the Gospel to mixed crowds, black and white, in many different Protestant churches in the eastern part of the United States and lower Canada—wherever she found people hungry to hear the Word of God.

Lee was an emotional preacher, one who invited God's Spirit to flow through her and guide her words when she preached. Many were moved closer to God by her preaching style. She held prayer meetings wherever she went, prayed for people, and asked them to pray for her.

Jarena Lee's determination to preach the Gospel was an example to other women that they too could be preachers. Today, thanks to Jarena and others like her, women fill many roles in the church as group leaders, teachers, counselors, and pastors.

Preach the Word of God. Preach it when it is easy and people want to listen and when it is hard and people do not want to listen. Preach it all the time.
2 Timothy 4:2

Katharina Luther
{1499–1552}

The Great Escape

When you have no words, the Bible can help you pray. The Psalms are full of prayers. Katharina Luther knew this when she prayed a prayer found in Psalm 31:1–2: "O Lord, in You I have found a safe place. . . . Set me free, because You do what is right and good. Turn Your ear to me, and be quick to save me. Be my rock of strength, a strong place to keep me safe."

Katharina's story begins in sixteenth-century Germany at a time when Protestants fought to break away from the Catholic Church. Katharina was a Catholic nun who wanted to escape from her convent. But leaving wasn't allowed. If caught, she could spend her life in prison.

One of the most well-known Protestant leaders then was Martin Luther. Katharina liked his ideas, so she secretly contacted him and asked for his help.

Luther put together a plan. The night before Easter in 1523, Katharina escaped by hiding in an empty fish barrel on a merchant's wagon. She was brought to Luther, who didn't know what to do with her. It was a crime to hide her. Her family didn't want her. The only option left was for Martin to marry her.

Katharina and Martin grew to love each other deeply. She became a strong woman who encouraged other women by example. She wasn't afraid to speak up and speak out for what she believed. She stood by her husband and helped as he led Protestants to form a new church.

Katharina had prayed a prayer from the Psalms, and God heard. He set her free and provided her with even more—a husband, children, and a good life.

Read the Psalms in your Bible. See if you can find some prayers.

BE FILLED WITH THE SPIRIT, SPEAKING TO ONE ANOTHER WITH PSALMS, HYMNS, AND SONGS FROM THE SPIRIT. SING AND MAKE MUSIC FROM YOUR HEART TO THE LORD.
EPHESIANS 5:18–19 NIV

Mary Lyon
{1797–1849}

Mary's Hilltop Prayer

Nineteen-year-old Mary Lyon walked home from church, taking the long way on the dirt road, walking slowly, thinking about the sermon her pastor delivered about God's love. As Mary came near the little cottage on her family's one-hundred-acre farm in Massachusetts, she decided not to go inside. Instead, she walked up a nearby hill so she could spend time alone with God. On the hilltop, Mary looked out at the faraway mountains, the valley, and plains. She looked down at her little village and thought of all God had made. Her heart overflowed with peace. Mary prayed, giving her life to God and asking Him to guide her forever.

Mary lived when it was believed women didn't need much education. She was blessed to have more schooling than most girls. That led to a job teaching in a tiny, one-room schoolhouse. She was a good teacher, but she felt God leading her to become even better. Mary wanted, more than anything else, to be certain girls got a good education.

She raised money to start her own school, a college for girls. She named it Mount Holyoke. In Mary's school, girls learned science, math, and other subjects. But Mary wanted her students to know about God too. She required them to attend church and Bible study. She also set aside quiet time so her girls could be alone and pray. Her school was successful and grew!

Today Mary Lyon is remembered as a leader in women's education and founder of the first women's college in the United States. Mount Holyoke still exists as a women's college. Women from all over the world have been educated there. Many graduates of Mount Holyoke became leaders who went on to inspire others—all thanks to God, Mary, and her hilltop prayer.

- -

We are sure that if we ask anything that He wants us to have, He will hear us.
1 John 5:14

Bailee Madison
{1999-}

"It's Not about Me"

Bailee Madison has been acting since she was a little girl. Among her many film credits are *Bridge to Terabithia* and *Letters to God*. Becoming famous at such a young age might be enough to make some kids stuck up and unfriendly—but not Bailee. When she started earning success as an actor and felt that was really cool, her mom told her, "You have to stay humble, Bailee." The young performer listened to her mom, and she knows that her success isn't about her. It's about God. He chose for her to act. She also understands that God might lead her down a totally different path someday. And Bailee is okay with that. She has learned God has a reason for everything.

When she has to act, Bailee says she isn't nervous. She prays, asking God to take any anxiety away and let His words flow through her. She says to Him, "Let me feel You inside of me."

Bailee has faced challenges in her career working with difficult directors and having scenes she really wanted to perform taken away from her. There were times when she went home crying and asking God, "Why me?" God helped her through those times.

Prayer is important to Bailee. She talks with God as she would talk to her dad on earth. She tells God how she feels, and she knows He loves her. Bailee has committed herself to God, and she believes He will always take care of her.

Bailee Madison's goals are to do nice things and help people. But she doesn't want it to be about her. She wants it to be about God. That is what it means to be humble.

Are you humble when you do something awesome or win an award? Think about Bailee's story and practice making success not about you but about God.

HUMBLE YOURSELVES BEFORE THE LORD, AND HE WILL LIFT YOU UP.
JAMES 4:10 NIV

Catherine Marshall
{1914–83}

Helpless No More

When Catherine Wood attended college in Georgia, she met a young Scottish preacher named Peter Marshall. The two got married, and Catherine settled into life as a preacher's wife. Before long, Peter was asked to pastor a church in Washington, DC.

Catherine Marshall had no idea how famous her husband would become. People loved his sermons. The US Senate asked Peter to be their chaplain, and he served there until he suffered a sudden heart attack and died when he was just forty-six years old.

When Peter died, Catherine became a single mom raising their nine-year-old son. Catherine Marshall prayed a lot after her husband's death. She said, "My most spectacular answers to prayers have come when I was so helpless, so out of control as to be able to do nothing at all for myself."

God listened as Catherine poured out her grief to Him and laid her helpless feelings before Him. She had no idea what would happen next, but God knew.

He led Catherine to write a book. She put together some of Peter's best sermons. It instantly became a bestseller. That book was the first of many Catherine wrote. For the rest of her life, she penned bestselling nonfiction books, biographies, and novels for adults, children, and teens. One of her books, *A Man Called Peter*, was made into a movie, and her book *Christy* became a television series.

Only God knows what He has planned for you. There will be times when you might feel helpless, like Catherine. That's a normal part of life. If you ask God to lead you out of that helplessness, He will. Just pray and trust Him to show you what to do next. Aren't you excited to see what He has planned for your future?

"AND NOW, LORD, WHAT DO I WAIT FOR? MY HOPE IS IN YOU."
PSALM 39:7

Martha

{JOHN 11:1-45}

She Believed

Jesus made friends wherever he went. People loved listening to His wise words and seeing the miraculous things He did.

We know He had three very close friends, Lazarus and his sisters, Mary and Martha. The Bible says Jesus loved them, and He enjoyed spending time at their house. They all trusted Jesus, believing He would be there to help whenever they needed Him.

One day when Jesus was not nearby, Lazarus got very sick. His sisters sent for Jesus, but Jesus did not come right away. In the meantime, Lazarus died. Four days later, after Lazarus was buried, Jesus showed up. A huge boulder had been rolled in front of Lazarus's tomb, sealing his body inside.

Martha said, "Lord, if You had been here, my brother would not have died. I know even now God will give You whatever You ask" (vv. 21–22). She trusted that Jesus was God's Son, capable of doing anything, even bringing Lazarus back to life.

Jesus did a miracle that day, something unbelievable. He raised Lazarus from the dead. The stone was rolled away from the tomb, and Lazarus walked out—as alive as ever! It had been Jesus' plan all along to wait and then do something amazing.

Sometimes when you pray, Jesus seems far away. But always you can be certain He will show up. His Spirit is with you all the time, quietly helping with whatever you need. When you pray, tell Him, "Jesus, I believe in You. I know You are with me. You can fix any problem I have. I trust You to do it Your way and in Your time. Amen."

THE LORD IS GOOD TO THOSE WHO WAIT FOR HIM, TO THE ONE WHO LOOKS FOR HIM.
IT IS GOOD THAT ONE SHOULD BE QUIET AND WAIT FOR THE SAVING POWER OF THE LORD.
LAMENTATIONS 3:25-26

Mary, Mother of Jesus
{Luke 1:28-35, 46-55}

Give Thanks!

God has a plan for everything, and His plans are always perfect. His best plan, so far, is giving us Jesus.

God knew humans were not strong enough on their own to always resist sin. Sin has no place in heaven. And because God wants all people to get into heaven someday, He sent His Son, Jesus, to help.

He planned to send Jesus to earth as a baby, and He chose a girl named Mary to give birth to Jesus. An angel told Mary that the baby Jesus would soon be growing inside her. The baby had no earthly father. He was the Son of God!

Mary didn't know why God had chosen her. The angel only said, "You are honored very much. You are a favored woman. The Lord is with you. You are chosen from among many women" (v. 28).

Imagine what went through Mary's thoughts! God had chosen her to help bring Jesus into the world. The awesomeness of it overwhelmed her. What did Mary do? She thanked God. She said, "My heart sings with thanks for my Lord. And my spirit is happy in God, the One Who saves from the punishment of sin. . . . He Who is powerful has done great things for me. His name is holy" (vv. 46–47, 49).

Mary's story reminds us to thank God for His goodness. When you pray, remember to thank Him for the wonderful things He does. Stop right now and think about something God did for you today. Then say a little thank-you prayer.

Be full of joy all the time. Never stop praying. In everything give thanks. This is what God wants you to do because of Christ Jesus.
1 Thessalonians 5:16–18

Mary of Bethany
{Luke 10:38-42}

It Takes Two

Jesus was on His way to visit Mary and Martha. The sisters looked forward to His visits, and when they heard He was coming, they got busy. There was plenty to do. Along with getting their house in order, Martha planned a delicious meal for their Friend. The two women worked side by side, helping each other. But when Jesus arrived, Mary stopped working. While Martha cooked, Mary sat with Jesus. They talked, and she listened carefully to everything He said.

This made Martha unhappy. "Jesus," she said, "do You see that my sister is not helping me? Tell her to help me."

Jesus answered, "Martha, you are worried and troubled about many things. Only a few things are important, even just one. Mary has chosen the good thing. It will not be taken away from her" (vv. 40-42).

Think about what Jesus said. The most important thing you can do, the best thing, is having uninterrupted talks with Him.

Prayer is talking *with* Jesus. It is a two-way take-turns activity. You talk to Him while He listens, and then *you* listen to *Him*.

Mary understood the importance of talking with Jesus. Nothing got in the way of her time with Him. She set everything aside and turned all her attention to their conversation.

You can learn to be like Mary. When you pray, practice shutting out anything that might distract you. Focus on your prayer. Speak to Jesus, but then be still. When you learn to quiet yourself and listen, you will hear His voice in your heart, guiding your thoughts and leading you to do what is right.

. . . .

"Call to Me, and I will answer you."
JEREMIAH 33:3

MIRIAM
{EXODUS 15:20-21}

Praise God!

Maybe you've heard someone say, "Praise God!" Praise is a joyful prayer of thanksgiving. It might be the best kind of prayer, because praise is all about God. When we praise Him, we don't ask for anything. Praise is honoring God for only one reason—for being our one and only amazing God!

The Bible holds many examples of praise. One of the first is Miriam's story.

Miriam was Moses' sister. She was with him when he led the Israelites out of Egypt where Pharaoh held them as slaves.

As Moses led the Israelites away, Pharaoh's army chased them all the way to the Red Sea. When Moses and the Israelites got there, God parted the sea and opened up a dry pathway for them to walk through. When they were safely on the other side, God closed the path, and the sea swallowed up Pharaoh's army!

Miriam led the women in praise. "Miriam said to them, 'Sing to the Lord, for He is praised for His greatness. He has thrown the horse and horseman into the sea' " (v. 21). The women were so filled with joyfulness that they played tambourines, sang, and danced, praising God for His goodness.

Have you ever been so happy that you jumped up and down? Or maybe you danced or sang a song? When something good happens to you, God allowed that to happen. He is the One who deserves praise. God loves praise! If you are so happy that you want to sing and dance your praises to Him, He loves that too.

Get in the habit of praising God—not just for what He does, but especially for who He is!

I WILL BE GLAD AND FULL OF JOY BECAUSE OF YOU.
I WILL SING PRAISE TO YOUR NAME, O MOST HIGH.
PSALM 9:2

MONICA OF HIPPO
{331-87}

Augustine's Mom

The story of Monica and her son, Augustine, happened long ago. But the same kind of story might be told in families today.

Augustine's mom, Monica, believed in Jesus. She raised her son to be Christian. But as Augustine grew older, he had his own ideas about religion. He left Hippo (the place in Africa where they lived) to follow a new religion created by a guy named Mani, who called himself the "Apostle of Light." In today's world, you might say Augustine joined a cult. Moms worry about their kids, and Monica was no different. She had to do something! But Augustine was old enough to make his own choices. She couldn't go where he was and take him home. So Monica turned to Jesus.

She prayed and prayed, day after day. Monica cried too because nothing was changing with Augustine. For nine years, Monica prayed. She asked others to pray for her son too. Then things got worse. Augustine went even farther away from home to teach philosophy in Rome. He was smart and on his way to becoming one of the greatest philosophers of his time. But still he wasn't a Christian.

While in Rome, Augustine left the cult. This was good news! But he continued to struggle with his ideas about Jesus. Monica kept on praying and relying on Bible promises. She eventually went to be with him, to nudge him toward Christianity. Finally, Monica received the best gift ever. After seventeen years of praying for her son, Augustine accepted Jesus into his heart. And that's not all. He became one of the greatest Christians in history!

Monica's story reminds us to never stop praying. God hears, and in His time, He will make things right.

PRAY CONTINUALLY, AND GIVE THANKS WHATEVER HAPPENS.
1 THESSALONIANS 5:17-18 NCV

LOTTIE MOON
{1840-1912}

With a Little Help from Her Friends

Lottie Moon grew up in Virginia in the 1840s. Her family was Baptist, and Lottie's mom made sure Lottie knew about Jesus. But Lottie didn't care. She wasn't sure she believed in Jesus, and she was rebellious. Lottie was smart. She did well in school, but she caused a lot of trouble. Her Christian friends put Lottie on their prayer list, asking God to save her from sin. God answered their prayers. Lottie lay awake one night thinking about her behavior. She knew she needed Jesus, so she prayed all night and put her faith and trust in Him.

Lottie's love for the Lord led her to missionary work in China, where few people believed in Jesus. She found it difficult to encourage them to accept Christ as their Savior. So Lottie prayed, and God revealed to her that she needed to be their friend and to *show*, instead of tell, them how to be Christians.

She moved to a small village in the Chinese countryside and tried to be friendly with people there. Often Lottie baked cookies. When children smelled the delicious treats baking, they went to her house—and before long Lottie met their mothers. As she made friends, the people began listening to Lottie's stories about Jesus. Many prayed and accepted Him into their hearts.

Lottie Moon stayed in China most of her life and encouraged other missionaries to come there. Long after her death, she continues to help support missionaries around the world through the Southern Baptist Lottie Moon Christmas Offering.

None of what she accomplished might have happened if Lottie's friends hadn't prayed for her.

Maybe you know a kid in school who causes trouble. Pray for him or her. You never know—God might use that person in an amazing way.

"BUT I TELL YOU, LOVE THOSE WHO HATE YOU. {RESPECT AND GIVE THANKS FOR THOSE WHO SAY BAD THINGS TO YOU. DO GOOD TO THOSE WHO HATE YOU.} PRAY FOR THOSE WHO DO BAD THINGS TO YOU AND WHO MAKE IT HARD FOR YOU."
MATTHEW 5:44

HANNAH MORE
{1745–1833}

Hannah's Sunday School

Hannah More is most often remembered as an English poet and writer. She wrote poems and plays about slavery and encouraged women to join the antislavery movement in England. Hannah was deeply concerned about others and especially about education for the poor. She prayed and practiced a strong Christian faith. "A sincere love of God will make us thankful when our prayers are granted, and patient and cheerful when they are denied," she said.

A friend told Hannah about conditions in a nearby village called Cheddar. The people there were poor, and they didn't know God. Hannah went to see for herself. She found only one Bible in the village, and it was used to prop up a flowerpot!

Hannah decided to start a Sunday school there. She became one of the first youth group leaders in history. She understood that to stay interested, children needed activities. So Hannah tried to make Sunday school fun. She used singing and encouraged her students to do community projects. Together they built a village oven for baking breads and puddings.

Her Sunday school methods were so successful that Hannah wrote down her ideas so others could learn from her. She shared that Sunday school needs to be entertaining, and lessons have to fit the ages of the different children who attend. She wrote about the importance of using kindness with children. Hannah even suggested that children be given little rewards for attending Sunday school and learning scripture. The idea of rewarding children for learning wasn't popular back then. But Hannah More's ideas caught on. They led to many more Sunday schools in the nineteenth century.

What is your favorite part of Sunday school? If you don't go to Sunday school, ask God to lead you there.

. . . .

JESUS SAID, "LET THE LITTLE CHILDREN COME TO ME. DO NOT STOP THEM.
THE HOLY NATION OF HEAVEN IS MADE UP OF ONES LIKE THESE."
MATTHEW 19:14

NaOMI
{rUTH 1:1-18}

Naomi's Unselfish Prayer

You will find Naomi's story in the book of Ruth. It begins like this: "In the days when there were judges to rule, there was a time of no food in the land. A certain man of Bethlehem in Judah went to visit the land of Moab with his wife and his two sons. The name of the man was Elimelech. His wife's name was Naomi" (Ruth 1:1-2).

Drought caused the crops in Bethlehem to die. There was nothing to eat, so Naomi's family moved to Moab. They lived happily for a while until Naomi's husband, Elimelech, died. Still, she had her sons, Mahlon and Chilion, to help her. The boys grew up and married women from Moab. This was good! Now Naomi had two more helpers.

But trouble came. Naomi's sons died. *Both* of them! (The Bible doesn't tell us how.) This left Naomi and her daughters-in-law, Orpah and Ruth, with no strong men to help with the everyday heavy work.

Naomi decided to return to her homeland, Bethlehem.

Orpah and Ruth planned to go with her, but Naomi said, "No. Stay here in Moab, where you grew up." Then Naomi prayed an unselfish prayer, asking God to show the women kindness. She was willing to give up the only companions she had so they could have a good life in their homeland. She asked God to bless them!

An unselfish prayer like Naomi's is music to God's ears. Jesus said we should ask God for what we want. He even encouraged it! So, when you pray, it is perfectly fine to ask. But along with asking for yourself, remember Naomi's prayer, and ask God to meet the needs of others.

Pray for the things that are needed. You must watch and keep on praying. remember to pray for all christians.
EPHESIANS 6:18

FLORENCE NIGHTINGALE
{1820–1910}

History's Most Famous Nurse

Courage and compassion are two words that might best describe the character of Florence Nightingale. By age sixteen, Florence was greatly concerned about the sick and poor people living in her village. It was obvious to Florence that nursing was her calling, but her wealthy parents disagreed. They thought a nursing career was below her social standing.

But Florence was strong-willed and determined and felt God was calling her to become a nurse. So she enrolled in nursing school despite her parents' protests. Once Florence was finished with her training and began working as a nurse, she was disgusted at the unsanitary conditions in many hospitals. She made some radical changes to help prevent the spread of germs in hospitals and make the environment safer and better for patients. Her bosses noticed, and so did many others.

War broke out in 1853, and Britain's secretary of war asked Florence to gather a team of nurses to help care for British soldiers in the military hospitals. The conditions there were horrible. Bugs and rodents ran throughout the filthy halls among the patients. The nurses didn't even have the supplies they needed. Florence prayed, asking God to supply for their needs. And she demanded that the place be cleaned up. Then she got busy caring for the men day and night.

Florence made it her life's mission to improve the poor conditions in hospitals and to make sure patients were well cared for. She became famous for her work. Before she died, Florence made notes to help those in charge of training nurses. And in her notes, among other things, she stressed how important it is for nurses to make time to pray.

Scheduling prayer time was important to Florence. And it should be important for all of us. Do you set aside time to pray every day?

. . . .

DEAR FRIEND, I PRAY THAT YOU ARE DOING WELL IN EVERY WAY.
I PRAY THAT YOUR BODY IS STRONG AND WELL EVEN AS YOUR SOUL IS.
3 JOHN 2

FLANNERY O'CONNOR
{1925-64}

Author!

When Flannery O'Connor was twenty years old and a college student far from home, she kept a journal in which she drew and also wrote her prayers. She had a passion to write, and she prayed about it often. "Please help me, dear God, to be a good writer," she wrote in her journal.

People with different religious views surrounded Flannery. She was also aware of the sin and misery around her. She worried about losing her faith. "I dread, oh Lord, losing my faith," she wrote. "My mind is not strong. It is a prey to all sorts of intellectual quackery."

She wanted to write in a way that led others to God, so Flannery asked Him to give her stories to write. When her stories were published, she gave God all the credit. Her stories are not what you might expect from a Christian author. They centered on sin and misery. Her writing was dark, violent, even shocking. She wanted readers to realize they needed God's grace. "All human nature. . .resists grace because grace changes us and the change is painful," Flannery said. She sometimes questioned and worried that she was doing the right thing. "Please don't let me have to scrap the story because it turns out to mean more wrong than right," she wrote in her journal.

Flannery O'Connor became one of the greatest short story writers of the twentieth century. We can learn from her the importance of praying and relying on God. Flannery made Christ the center of her everything. Maybe that's why she became a successful author.

The theme of many of Flannery's stories is God's grace—His unconditional love even when we don't deserve it. Have you experienced His grace?

However, I consider my life worth nothing to me; my only aim is to finish the race and complete the task the Lord Jesus has given me— the task of testifying to the good news of God's grace.
Acts 20:24 niv

PHOEBE PALMER
{1807–74}

How Do You Feel?

Have you ever been confused about your feelings? You think you should feel a certain way, but you don't. And you say to yourself, *Is something wrong with me that I don't feel the way I'm supposed to?*

Phoebe Palmer had that problem. She had committed her life to Jesus, but she didn't feel any different. Salvation meant accepting that Jesus had died for her sins. It guaranteed she would be with Him in heaven after she died. How awesome was that? Phoebe's religion taught that salvation came with tears of joy and excitement. It made you so happy, you wanted to get up and dance. But Phoebe didn't feel any of those things. She was certain that she had accepted Jesus as her Lord and Savior, but her experience felt matter-of-fact. Phoebe decided something was missing. Where was all the emotion that was supposed to come from salvation?

She spent years searching for that feeling. She asked God to help her, to lead her to some Bible verse that might explain her lack of emotion. Finally, Phoebe received an answer: she had been spending more time focusing on her feelings than on Jesus and her salvation.

That changed everything for Phoebe! She put Jesus first before herself, her family, and her feelings. She got involved in leading prayer meetings and preaching about her experience. Many received salvation because of her. God blessed Phoebe with energy to preach and write about the importance of salvation. He gave her strong feelings to serve others and lead them to accepting Jesus into their hearts.

Maybe you are like Phoebe. Some people feel things more strongly than others. If you are confused about your feelings, remember her story. Ask God for help.

FOR BY HIS LOVING-FAVOR YOU HAVE BEEN SAVED FROM THE PUNISHMENT OF SIN THROUGH FAITH. IT IS NOT BY ANYTHING YOU HAVE DONE. IT IS A GIFT OF GOD.
EPHESIANS 2:8

Moriah Smallbone {Peters}
{1992-}

A Holy Collision

American Idol had rejected Christian singer Moriah Peters. It wasn't because of her talent but because she shared that she was Christian and was saving her first kiss for marriage. That rejection was God's plan. Within hours of her audition, Moriah was led to someone who would launch her career as a Christian solo artist.

But after a while, Moriah grew weary of going solo. She searched for something new. Starting a business might be her next step. Or maybe acting or going back to school. Moriah felt unsettled and unsure.

While on a trip to Israel, she asked God what she should do. "I know the next step isn't going to be in music," she told Him.

Oh, but it was! Moriah felt God telling her He wasn't done with her music career yet. He was going to lead her to a new project involving her bandmates.

So Moriah followed where God led her. She teamed with former bandmates, Jesi Jones and Julie Melucci, to form a new band called TRALA. Together they wrote songs from their hearts. Then they produced their songs and released them as singles.

TRALA named their first single "Holy Collision." Moriah explains a holy collision as something unexpected, or maybe unwanted. God's answer to her prayer in Israel was certainly a holy collision! Their song got more than sixty-seven thousand streams on Spotify in its first six weeks. TRALA was, and is, a success.

None of it was supposed to happen. It wasn't Moriah's plan—it was God's, just as her *American Idol* rejection had been.

Maybe you have tried your best at something but failed. Don't dwell on failure. Instead, remember Moriah's prayer. Ask God what He wants you to do next.

IF YOU DO NOT HAVE WISDOM, ASK GOD FOR IT. HE IS ALWAYS READY
TO GIVE IT TO YOU AND WILL NEVER SAY YOU ARE WRONG FOR ASKING.

JAMES 1:5

Pandita Ramabai
{1858–1922}

Mistress of Wisdom

Pandita Ramabai's name means "Mistress of Wisdom." You will learn from her story that all wisdom comes from the one and only true God.

Pandita was born into a Hindu family in India. Her family bowed down to idols and worshipped gods, goddesses, trees, and animals. They traveled to temples and holy places where the gods and goddesses were supposed to live. While searching for help from these gods, they became poor. Pandita's father, mother, and sister died of starvation. Only Pandita and her brother lived.

As a young woman, she could relate to the troubles she saw all around her. Pandita lost faith in her Hindu religion. The gods had not answered her family's prayers. It was about this time that she met some English missionaries who gave her a Bible. Pandita read it. She learned a lot about Christianity, but she wasn't ready to put her faith in Jesus.

After Pandita got a scholarship to study medicine in England, she saw Christianity at work. Christians in England helped the poor. They were filled with the love of Jesus and the desire to serve others. Because of their example, Pandita discovered how much she needed Jesus herself, and she gave her life to Him.

Jesus became her teacher. Pandita prayed and traveled the world, sharing her faith with others. In India she started Christian "salvation missions." She set up schools, orphanages, and also women's shelters to help Indian women learn to live fulfilling, independent Christian lives.

Pandita Ramabai's story is a reminder that there is just one true God. She had learned that trusting Jesus led to everything good. He helped her serve others, and Pandita felt sure that when her work on earth was done, she would have forever life with Him in heaven.

"Have no gods other than me."
Exodus 20:3

HELEN STEINER RICE
{1900-1981}

Helen's Poems and Prayers

When God sees a need, He uses His people to fill it. It might not happen right away. God knows the future, so He often prepares His people well in advance. When the perfect time arrives, God does something to put the right people in the right places at the right times. Helen Steiner Rice's story is an example.

When she was little, Helen enjoyed writing rhymes. As a Christian, she loved sharing God's love with her family. Helen was smart! Her teachers encouraged her to go to college. She wanted to become a congresswoman. But then something happened—something that sent Helen in a very different direction.

Her dad died. Helen was needed to help provide financial support for her mom and sister. So, instead of going to college, Helen went to work for the electric company. She did very well there, giving speeches about the advantages of electricity. After a few years, Helen moved on to work as an editor at the Gibson greeting card company. At Gibson, some of her rhyming poems became cards. The best of them were prayer-poems that inspired others to have faith in God.

In 1960 one of her poems, "The Priceless Gift of Christmas," was read on a popular television show. Almost overnight Helen became famous for her Christian poetry. The words she wrote touched people in the most difficult times of their lives and reminded them that God cared. Helen wrote poems and prayers that today are read by people all over the world.

Helen Steiner Rice died in 1981, but her words live on in greeting cards and books. God knew that people needed faith and encouragement. He had chosen Helen to reach others for Him, not just during her lifetime but long after she died.

THERE ARE MANY PLANS IN A MAN'S HEART, BUT IT IS THE LORD'S PLAN THAT WILL STAND.
PROVERBS 19:21

Darlene Deibler Rose
{1917-2004}

Whatever the Cost

Lord, I will go anywhere with you, no matter what it costs." Darlene prayed that prayer when she was just ten years old. She had no idea then where she would go with Jesus. She likely didn't remember that He often goes to provide help and comfort in the worst of circumstances.

At age nineteen, Darlene and her new husband, both American, traveled to the jungles of New Guinea to do mission work. For a while, things went well, but then World War II happened. Japanese soldiers came. They arrested Darlene and her husband and put them into separate prison camps. Darlene's husband died. She was accused of being a spy and tortured by the Japanese soldiers. They did terrible things to her and the other women and children in the camp. But through it all, Darlene knew that Jesus was there with her—with all of them. His presence brought her comfort. Other Christians were held captive with her, and they helped each other by praying together, quoting scripture, and singing hymns.

For much of the four years she was in prison, Darlene was often alone in a cell. Her mind drifted to "what-ifs." *What if I never go home? What if my parents are dead? What if. . .?* But always she prayed, and Jesus was there. Darlene learned to live in the moment and rely on Him for all her what-ifs.

When the war ended, Darlene returned home to America, grateful that God had taken her with Him into the worst of situations. She said those years in prison were the sweetest she'd ever known because she became certain that Jesus was always with her—whatever the cost. She had experienced the faithfulness of His never-ending love.

Think about it: would you be willing to go anywhere with Jesus?

"I am with you always, even to the end of the world."
MATTHEW 28:20

RUTH
{RUTH 1-4}

God Bless You!

Ruth's story was just beginning when Naomi told her to stay in her homeland. Ruth did something unselfish in return. She refused to allow Naomi to go home to Bethlehem alone. Ruth insisted on going with her. She told Naomi, "Do not beg me to leave you or turn away from following you. I will go where you go. I will live where you live. Your people will be my people. And your God will be my God." Ruth promised God that she would never leave Naomi for as long as she lived (1:16–17).

You have likely heard someone say, "God bless you!" It is a short prayer asking God to show goodness to the person being prayed for. "God bless you for your kindness. God bless you for your hard work. God bless you with good health. . . ."

When Naomi told Ruth and Orpah to stay in their homeland, she also asked God to bless them with His kindness. And that is exactly what God did! He blessed Ruth.

She went to Bethlehem with Naomi and met a handsome and rich man named Boaz. They fell in love, got married, and lived happily ever after—and Naomi along with them! (Read the book of Ruth in the Bible to learn more about their love story.) God even blessed Ruth with a son, an important part of God's future plan. The little boy grew up to be the grandfather to Israel's greatest king, King David!

From now on, when you say to someone "God bless you," remember that it is a prayer. You are asking God to show His goodness to someone.

Think about it. . .who can you ask God to bless today?

"MAY THE Lord BLESS YOU AND KEEP YOU. MAY THE Lord SHOW YOU HIS KINDNESS AND HAVE MERCY ON YOU. MAY THE Lord WATCH OVER YOU AND GIVE YOU PEACE."
NUMBERS 6:24–26 NCV

Salome
{Matthew 20:20-25}

A Mother's Prayer

Salome was mother to Jesus' disciples James and John. She felt pleased that Jesus had chosen her boys as His disciples. Just like moms today, she wanted the best for her kids. She was proud of her boys.

One day Jesus told His disciples that soon He would be arrested and sentenced to die. And then, three days later, God would raise Him to life again.

Salome believed Jesus was God's Son and that He would have a special king-like place in heaven. So she got on her knees in front of Him and prayed for a favor. She said, "Say that my two sons may sit, one at Your right side and one at Your left side, when You are King" (Matthew 20:21). Salome knew that someday her boys would die, and when their time came, she wanted her kids to have the best seats in heaven—sitting next to Jesus.

Jesus answered, "The places at My right side and at My left side are not Mine to give. Whoever My Father says will have those places" (Matthew 20:23). Then Jesus told Salome and His disciples that greatness does not come from how important you are. Greatness comes from serving others.

Salome's story teaches us that while it is awesome to win awards and to be the best at something, true greatness comes from doing for others. When you pray, ask Jesus to teach you to serve your family, church, community, and the world.

Salome and her boys continued to follow Jesus. We don't know who sits on either side of Jesus in heaven, but one day when we get there, we will find out.

"He who is greatest among you will be the one to care for you."
Matthew 23:11

DOROTHY Sayers
{1893–1957}

She Dared to Be Different

If you had known Dorothy Sayers, you would have noticed she had strong opinions, and she wasn't afraid to share them. She was a creative person, a writer, and was best known for her crime novels. Dorothy wrote her crime mysteries when women didn't write "that sort of book," and she became one of the greatest mystery writers of the twentieth century.

Dorothy lived in England. Her dad was a minister, and Dorothy grew up learning the importance of prayer and putting her faith in Jesus. She was a Christian, and she had strong opinions about that too. She used her stories to show readers there were consequences for choosing evil over good. Her words left readers thinking about things like guilt, conscience, and the need to be saved from making bad choices.

When Dorothy read the Gospels—the books of Matthew, Mark, Luke, and John that tell the story of Jesus—she looked beyond the Bible language that sometimes made the stories difficult to understand. She saw the people in the stories as people whom we can relate to right now.

She wrote a series of radio plays for children called *The Man Born to Be King*. They told Jesus' story in language that kids could understand. Some Christians disliked the idea of updating the Bible language and tried to stop the stories from being broadcast. But they were broadcast, and they became popular. Adults liked them too, and many people became interested in reading the Bible—thanks to Dorothy's plays.

Dorothy Sayers dared to be different. She used creative writing to share Jesus with others. Can you think of your own creative way of sharing Him with your family and friends?

IT HAS ALWAYS BEEN MY AMBITION TO PREACH THE GOSPEL
WHERE CHRIST WAS NOT KNOWN.
ROMANS 15:20 NIV

EDITH SCHAEFFER
{1914–2013}

L'Abri—the Shelter

At a youth group meeting, Edith heard someone say Jesus was not God's Son and the Bible was not God's Word. Edith knew better! She stood and disagreed with the speaker. At the same time, a boy across the room stood and disagreed too. That was how Edith met her future husband, Francis Schaeffer.

Edith and Francis married, and God blessed the Schaeffers with four children. The family went to Switzerland, where Edith and Francis could work as missionaries. They settled into a house in a quiet mountain valley. The Schaeffers began inviting the villagers' children into their home to learn about Jesus. But the village leaders didn't like the Schaeffers sharing their religious views. They told them to leave.

Edith and her husband moved their family to another village in the Swiss mountains. There they had freedom to open their home to anyone who wanted to come talk about God and have their questions answered. Francis and Edith asked God to send those who needed to know Him. God answered their prayer. People began hearing about the Schaeffers, and they came to stay as guests at the Schaeffers' L'Abri—the French word for "shelter."

Edith and Francis never judged those who came. Edith showed everyone the same love and hospitality. She was welcoming, warm, and nonjudgmental—the way Jesus is! She cooked, cleaned, and shared with guests the truth that God is real and ever-present in their everyday lives. The ministry at L'Abri grew, and it continues today, serving people of all ages.

Edith and Francis Schaeffer prayed an excellent prayer—one you should pray too. Ask God to send you people who need to know Him. Then you can be like Edith and tell them about Jesus!

My children, let us not love with words or in talk only. Let us love by what we do and in truth.
1 John 3:18

Lauren Scruggs
{1988–}

Triumph after Tragedy

December 3, 2011, began like an ordinary day for model and fashion blogger Lauren Scruggs. That evening Lauren and her mom went to their friends' house for dinner. Afterward, one of the friends, a pilot, asked Lauren if she would like to take a flight to see the Christmas lights from the air.

When Lauren got into the small plane, she felt a rush of fear. She didn't know why, but she thought something was going to happen. After the flight, Lauren felt relieved. She remembers getting out of the plane and her feet touching the ground—and that's all!

Lauren had walked into the plane's spinning propeller. She was badly injured. When she finally woke up in the hospital, Lauren discovered that she had lost her left eye and her left hand. She was in severe pain, but Lauren, a Christian, prayed and relied on God for comfort.

She had a long road ahead of her to get well again, but faith and prayer kept Lauren moving forward. Her dad read scriptures to her in the hospital. Her mom and sister stayed by her side. Lauren says she always felt that Jesus was there with her.

Her accident made Lauren aware of how many girls don't like something about their bodies. She wanted them to know that appearance doesn't define who they are. Lauren asked God how she could help.

Today Lauren runs an organization with the purpose of giving self-confidence to women who have lost arms or legs. She partners with a company that provides a skin-like covering for artificial arms and legs that make them look real. Lauren says the accident gave her a new purpose and that God's plan for her turned out to be really beautiful.

What can you learn from Lauren's story? Have you ever had a difficult time and God helped you get through it?

"WHEN YOU PASS THROUGH THE WATERS, I WILL BE WITH YOU. WHEN YOU PASS THROUGH THE RIVERS, THEY WILL NOT FLOW OVER YOU. WHEN YOU WALK THROUGH THE FIRE, YOU WILL NOT BE BURNED. THE FIRE WILL NOT DESTROY YOU."
ISAIAH 43:2

Ida Scudder
{1870–1960}

Missionary Doctor

Ida Scudder's family included many American missionary doctors in India. Her dad was one of them. Ida hadn't planned to become a missionary. She wanted to return to the States, go to college, and get married. But then her plans changed.

Her mom wasn't feeling well. Ida's dad needed Ida in India to help with their work. While working there, Ida saw three women die because they wanted to be treated by a woman doctor and there was none. At that moment, she felt it was God's plan that she become a doctor and help people in India. Ida prayed, "God, if You want me to stay in India, I will spend the rest of my life trying to help these women."

Ida got her medical degree in the States. Then she returned to India. Traveling in a cart pulled by oxen, she brought medical supplies and care to small villages. She prayed with the villagers. And when Ida grew tired, she prayed for strength: "Father, whose life is within me and whose love is ever about me, grant that this life may be maintained in my life today and every day, that with gladness of heart, without haste or confusion of thought, I may go about my daily tasks."

Ida Scudder set up clinics and a hospital and trained women to become nurses. She wanted to do even more for the Indian people, so she started a medical school where women, and later men, learned to be doctors.

Her school still exists today. The Christian Medical College and Hospital is one of the top-ranked medical schools in India. Its motto came from Ida: *Not to be ministered unto, but to minister.* What do you think that means? What did you learn about prayer from Ida's story?

"For I was hungry and you gave me food to eat. I was thirsty and you gave me water to drink. I was a stranger and you gave me a room."
Matthew 25:35

Mary Slessor
{1848-1915}

Risk Taker

Mary Slessor, a Scottish missionary in Africa, dared to go to faraway places where native African tribes lived. Few missionaries had the courage to go there, especially women. They feared they wouldn't survive. Superstition, as well as belief in demons, spirits, and false gods, existed everywhere among the tribes.

Many of the tribespeople were mistreated because of the false beliefs. But that didn't stop Mary from stepping in to help. In fact, she believed her purpose was to show mercy to the people. And so, with God's help, she took action.

Mary opened up a house where some of the tribespeople who were abandoned by their tribe—or even left to die—could be cared for. She welcomed many women and children. She cared for the children as though they were her very own.

She knew that if she wanted to help make a difference and show them the love of Jesus, she needed to live among the tribes. So Mary asked God to lead her and give her strength. She prayed, "Lord, the task is impossible for me but not for You. Lead the way, and I will follow."

She went deep into the jungle, knowing she was risking her life. Mary learned the tribe's language. She wasn't afraid to speak up and let them know when she disagreed with their ways. Amazingly, she became their friend. She participated in their good customs. She laughed with them and shared meals with them. The tribespeople eventually accepted her and also had respect and even love for her. Mary taught them about the Lord, and even when they were not accepting of what she had to say, she showed them nothing but kindness.

Think about it: if God asked you to risk your life to tell others about Jesus, would you be like Mary and obey?

"I am not worried about this. I do not think of my life as worth much, but I do want to finish the work the Lord Jesus gave me to do. My work is to preach the good news of God's loving-favor."
Acts 20:24

AMANDA BERRY SMITH
{1837–1915}

※※※※※

"Lord, I Am Willing to Go"

A manda Berry Smith talked to God all the time. One day she asked Him for direction in her life, and she sensed God saying, "Go, and I will go with you." But go where?

In her own words: "I was sitting with my eyes closed in silent prayer. . . . As I opened my eyes. . .I seemed to see a beautiful star. . .and I said, 'Lord, is that what you want me to see? If so, what else?' And then I leaned back and closed my eyes. Just then I saw a large letter G, and I said, 'Lord, do you want me to read in Genesis or in Galatians? Lord, what does this mean?' Just then I saw the letter O. I said, 'Why, that means go.' And I said, 'What else?' And a voice distinctly said to me, 'Go preach.'"

It was almost unheard of for an American woman to preach in Amanda's time, especially a black woman. Amanda knew she would face prejudice. But she answered God's call and preached the Word of God. She began preaching at religious meetings in the States. Then Amanda traveled overseas and preached in Great Britain, India, and Africa.

God had one more special task for her, this time back in the States. There was much discrimination then against African American children who were orphans. Amanda raised enough money to open an orphanage where children would be well cared for. To earn enough to keep the orphanage open, she ran a small newspaper. Her orphanage provided a home for up to thirty children at a time.

Amanda Berry Smith had been born a slave. God gave her freedom. And when He gave her a mission, she obeyed. "Lord, I am willing to go."

Are you willing to obey and say yes when God tells you to go?

•••

"NOW WHO IS WILLING TO GIVE HIMSELF AND BE SET APART TODAY TO THE LORD?"
1 CHRONICLES 29:5

HANNAH WHITALL SMITH
{1832–1911}

Good Enough?

Hannah Whitall Smith tried her best to be good, but she failed. She grew up in a home with strict rules about how to behave and work to please God. But sometimes Hannah messed up. She felt angry with herself. She felt she needed to try even harder to be perfect. Praying for forgiveness wasn't enough.

As Hannah tried harder, she didn't feel a deep love for God. She felt worthless; nothing she did felt good enough. Hannah wondered if God even existed.

When she was a young woman in her thirties, God led Hannah to Christians who had ideas different from hers. They seemed more joyful and not burdened by the thought that they could overcome sin. Hannah tells about it in her own words:

> I asked them their secret, and they replied, "It is simply in ceasing from all efforts of ours and in trusting the Lord to make us holy."
>
> "What!" I said "Do you really mean that you have ceased from your own efforts altogether. . .and that you do nothing but trust the Lord?"
>
> "Yes," was the reply, "the Lord does it all. We abandon ourselves to Him. We do not even try to live our lives ourselves. . .and He lives in us. He works in us."

Hannah Whitall Smith had learned the secret to a happy Christian life—God's grace. This means not getting the punishment you deserve. Jesus came to take the punishment for us. Thanks to Him, God loves and forgives us even when we mess up. Finally, Hannah felt free. She knew she was good enough!

Everyone messes up. When you mess up, remember Hannah's story: God loves you anyway. Ask Him to forgive you.

HE ANSWERED ME, "I AM ALL YOU NEED. I GIVE YOU MY LOVING-FAVOR.
MY POWER WORKS BEST IN WEAK PEOPLE." I AM HAPPY TO BE WEAK
AND HAVE TROUBLES SO I CAN HAVE CHRIST'S POWER IN ME.
2 CORINTHIANS 12:9

BONNIE ST. JOHN
{1964–}

Talking with God

Maybe you have heard of Bonnie St. John. She was the first African American woman to win medals in the Winter Paralympics—an international event where athletes with physical disabilities compete in winter sports. She took home one silver and two bronze medals while skiing on just one leg.

When Bonnie was five years old, doctors amputated her right leg because of a birth defect. Living with one leg taught Bonnie patience while she learned to do things that people with both legs found easy.

Bonnie worked hard. She did well in school and at almost everything she tried, but she had troubles too. Bad things had happened in her life that Bonnie couldn't forget. All the good things she experienced couldn't make up for those bad memories. She couldn't find joy in her heart.

She believed in God, and she knew it was good to pray. But for Bonnie, prayer was more an everyday exercise than really talking with God. As she began letting go of her bad feelings, Bonnie discovered a new way of talking with Him. She prayed all day, little prayers, talking with God just as she would with a friend. Bonnie learned that prayer feels good. If she gave her troubles to God, He helped her find joy. One day when she was about to deliver a speech to a big crowd, Bonnie prayed, and she imagined Jesus line dancing! She thought maybe He was trying to teach her to enjoy life instead of worrying or being afraid.

One thing Bonnie discovered is that everyone talks with God differently. Think about how you pray. Does praying make you feel closer to God? If not, maybe you should change how you pray. Ask your Christian friends to tell you how they pray.

WE DO NOT KNOW HOW TO PRAY AS WE SHOULD. BUT THE SPIRIT HIMSELF SPEAKS TO GOD FOR US, EVEN BEGS GOD FOR US WITH DEEP FEELINGS THAT WORDS CANNOT EXPLAIN.
ROMANS 8:26 NCV

Betty Stam
{1906-34}

Betty's Prayer

As a young woman, Betty wrote this prayer: "Lord, I give up all my own plans and purposes, all my own desires and hopes, and accept Thy will for my life. I give myself, my life, my all utterly to Thee to be Thine forever. . . . Use me as Thou wilt, send me where Thou wilt, and work out Thy will in my life at any cost now and forever."

Years later Betty and her husband, John, went to China to do mission work. It was a time when Communists plotted to overthrow the Chinese government. The Communists hated Christians, and missionaries were in danger.

After Betty and John had been in China awhile and they had a six-month-old daughter, word came that Communist soldiers were nearby. Soldiers arrived at their door before they were able to escape. Instead of reacting in fear and anger, Betty welcomed the soldiers with the same kindness Jesus might have. The soldiers kidnapped Betty, John, and their baby. They were put in prison, and the Communists demanded a ransom—$20,000—for their release. Betty and her husband knew that if their mission headquarters paid a ransom, it would only encourage more kidnappings of Christians. Although the Stams were treated like criminals for being Christians, they had a deep peace in their hearts because they knew that if they died for their faith, their service to God was worthwhile.

Sadly, Betty's story doesn't have a good ending. Her baby's life was spared, but the Communists murdered Betty and her husband. Their story spread around the world and touched many hearts. It even encouraged others to become missionaries themselves and continue the work Betty and John had begun.

Reread Betty's prayer. What do you think about her words? What can you learn from them?

. . . .

"DO NOT BE AFRAID OF THEM WHO KILL THE BODY.
THEY ARE NOT ABLE TO KILL THE SOUL."
MATTHEW 10:28

EDITH STEIN
{1891–1942}

A Christian Jew

Edith Stein was born in 1891 into a Jewish family in Poland. Her family believed in God, and at home Edith was taught about the Jewish faith. But by the time she reached her teens, Edith had given up praying. She searched for answers. She didn't think God was real.

Her search led Edith to a college in Germany to study philosophy—different ideas about how and why people, the world, and the universe exist. She was an excellent student. In her studies, she learned about different religions, and Edith became interested in the Catholic faith. But still she didn't believe in God.

One day Edith saw a young woman come from the marketplace and enter a Catholic church to pray. Edith was surprised by how informal it seemed. The woman simply went inside the empty church to have a quiet conversation with God. As Edith thought about that, she decided to read the New Testament.

God opened Edith's heart to the truth. She discovered that she *did* believe in God. She believed in Jesus too! Edith Stein became a Christian. She understood that God had her life all planned out.

Edith became a nun and served God and others through her work. But sadly her life ended during World War II. Edith saw German soldiers arresting Jewish people for no reason other than that they were Jews. "I never knew that people could be like this, neither did I know that my brothers and sisters would have to suffer like this. . . . I pray for them every hour," Edith said. But Edith, born a Jew, didn't escape the evil. The soldiers put her into a Nazi concentration camp, and she died there. Because Edith was a Christian, we know she has forever life in heaven.

Have you committed your life to Jesus so that you can have a "forever life" in heaven too?

....

"THIS IS LIFE THAT LASTS FOREVER. IT IS TO KNOW YOU, THE ONLY TRUE GOD, AND TO KNOW JESUS CHRIST WHOM YOU HAVE SENT."
JOHN 17:3

Harriet Beecher Stowe
{1811–96}

American Author

Most kids have heard an adult say, "You'll understand when you're older." If Harriet Beecher Stowe were here, she might tell you, "I long to put the experience of fifty years at once into your young lives, to give you at once the key to that treasure chamber, every gem of which has cost me tears and struggles and prayers, but you must work for these inward treasures yourselves."

Harriet was an American author who lived during the time when African Americans were slaves. She hated slavery. Harriet wrote a novel about it called *Uncle Tom's Cabin*, in which the main character, Tom, an African American slave, suffers terribly but never lets go of his Christian faith. The book made Harriet famous. It was banned in the South, and even today it is criticized for some of its language.

She said, "I did not write it. God wrote it. I merely did His dictation." Harriet saw herself as a servant of God. The idea for *Uncle Tom's Cabin* came to her during a church service. Harriet's husband urged her to write, telling her that her words could help the next generation.

Harriet prayed for slavery to end. She spoke out against slavery at a time when women often stayed silent. She knew slavery was anti-Christian. Along with working to end it in the United States, Harriet also urged women in England to fight against slavery. She wrote, "We appeal to you, as sisters, as wives, and as mothers, to raise your voices to your fellow-citizens, and your prayers to God for the removal of this affliction and disgrace from the Christian world."

Harriet would want you to remember her words. What have you learned from her story? What can you do today to help people get along?

"I give you a new law. You are to love each other. You must love each other as I have loved you."
JOHN 13:34

CLara Swain
{1834-1910}

Medical Missionary

Clara Swain was the first woman in the world to become a medical missionary. God's plan for Clara was for her to travel to India to help sick people there, especially women. In today's world, an American like Clara would get on an airplane and arrive in India in less than a day. But in the early 1800s, there were no airplanes. Clara traveled by ship, and she felt seasick most of the way.

When she got to India, her luggage hadn't arrived—and it wouldn't for another week. Transportation by horse and train also presented problems. She worried about tigers nearby. Clara didn't have enough food, and she was hungry. The journey was hard, but she went on, the prayers of her friends and family giving her strength. She was comforted to know that people were praying for her. Later she wrote letters and asked for more prayers, not only for herself but also for the sick people in India.

Along with caring for the sick, Clara trained female medical students to help her. Male doctors were not allowed to treat women back then. Clara worked long hours, treating more than thirteen hundred women in the first year. She helped heal them, and she gave them Bibles and told them about Jesus.

Clara decided that the women needed a hospital, so she asked God to make it happen. Miraculously, an Indian governor donated land, and three years later the first women's hospital in India opened its doors. It was named the Clara Swain Mission Hospital, and it still exists today, serving both women and men.

Think about how Clara was helped by her own prayers and the prayers of others. Do you have a friend with a special need? Ask God to help.

....

BROTHERS AND SISTERS, PRAY FOR US.
1 THESSALONIANS 5:25 NCV

CLARA SWAIN HOSPITAL

FIRST HOSPITAL FOR WOMEN IN ASIA
1870

JONI EARECKSON TADA
{1949-}

God Said No

Joni Eareckson Tada would probably tell you that there are things more important than being able to walk or use your hands. She knows! At age seventeen, Joni was in a diving accident that changed her life. She has been in a wheelchair for fifty years, unable to walk and with hands that barely work.

Knowing Jesus is the one thing that got Joni through the worst experience in her life. She prayed for God to heal her, but God said no. In time, Joni realized that not being healed was a gift. It deepened Joni's relationship with God, and it led her to start a ministry to help others, especially those with disabilities. Joni would probably share this with you: "I really would rather be in this wheelchair knowing Jesus as I do than be on my feet without Him."

Joni's ministry is called Joni and Friends. She hosts worldwide radio and television programs in which she shares God's Word and uplifting stories. She has written dozens of books, recorded albums of songs, and even starred in a movie about her life.

Even though life hasn't always been easy for Joni, she hasn't allowed it to keep her from living joyfully. Yes, she knows what it feels like to be depressed, to wish her accident had never happened. She's even doubted God. But she would tell you that He has never failed her or let her down. Instead, He uses Joni's life to help bring others out of their depression and into a joyful Christian life.

If God said no to your request for healing, what would you do?

· ·

"FOR MY THOUGHTS ARE NOT YOUR THOUGHTS,
AND MY WAYS ARE NOT YOUR WAYS," SAYS THE LORD.
ISAIAH 55:8

Elana Meyers Taylor
{1984-}

Representing Christ

Elana Meyers Taylor had her heart set on being an Olympian from the age of nine. She loved softball, and she decided that would lead to the summer Olympics. She gave softball her everything, heart and soul.

But when Elana got to college, her dream began to crumble. Her softball team was playing badly. Elana wasn't playing well either. She slipped into a depression, which led to an eating disorder. Elana decided that eating—or not—was the one thing in her life she could control. It was a bad decision.

She needed something deeper than herself to rely on. So Elana explored different religions. One day as she read a book on Buddhism, Elana started crying. She couldn't explain why, but at that moment she realized that the only One she needed was Jesus! The depression and eating disorder went away when Elana prayed and gave Jesus control of her life.

Her dream of the summer Olympics went away too. She tried out but didn't make the softball team. God had another plan. Bobsledding. Elana wasn't sure about it, but she tried out and made the US team! So far she has won three Olympic medals.

Today Elana relies on prayer and also Matthew 22:37–39, which says to love God with all your heart and to love others. That means loving her competitors, which isn't always easy. Elana helps them whenever she can, and she enjoys sharing her faith with them.

Elana Meyers Taylor is honored to represent the United States in the Olympics but even more honored to serve Jesus. She views her sport as a platform to spread His love. When she competes, Elana wants her behavior to reflect her faith. She is out there representing Christ.

"'You must love the Lord your God with all your heart and with all your soul and with all your mind.' This is the first and greatest of the laws. The second is like it, 'You must love your neighbor as you love yourself.'"
Matthew 22:37–39

Niki Taylor
{1975-}

Coming Apart

Niki Taylor wanted to become a marine biologist and someday have kids. When Niki was fourteen, her mother, a photographer, sent pictures of Niki to a modeling agency. Those led to Niki being on the cover of *Seventeen* magazine. More modeling jobs followed. At age seventeen, Niki became one of *Vogue*'s youngest cover girls. She was a teen millionaire by then, working steadily as a model. Her dream of becoming a marine biologist had taken a different turn.

Niki still dreamed of becoming a mother. She married at age eighteen and had twin boys when she was nineteen. She thought she had it all. Her life was a dream come true. But then everything began coming apart.

Niki and her younger sister, Krissy, were not only siblings but also best friends. On July 2, 1995, Niki found her sister unconscious in their parents' home. The paramedics were not able to save Krissy. She died of a rare heart condition. Krissy's death broke Niki's heart.

The next year, Niki's marriage ended in divorce. The anxiety caused Niki to take prescription drugs. She became addicted.

Niki considered herself a Christian, but other things had been more important. She needed God. So Niki surrounded herself with Christian friends who helped. She recommitted her life to Christ in 1998 and gave Him full control.

"When you are saved, it doesn't mean everything is perfect," Niki said. In 2001 she was injured in a terrible car accident that almost took her life. As a Christian, Niki approached that crisis differently. She said praying and faith brought her through several months in the hospital.

Today Niki is healthy, remarried, a business owner, mother to four beautiful kids, and best of all—God is at the center of her life.

What helped Niki get through the most difficult times of her life? What can you learn from her story?

GIVE ALL YOUR CARES TO THE LORD AND HE WILL GIVE YOU STRENGTH.
HE WILL NEVER LET THOSE WHO ARE RIGHT WITH HIM BE SHAKEN.
PSALM 55:22

corrie ten Boom
{1892-1983}

Corrie Takes the Wheel

Corrie ten Boom grew up in the Netherlands during World War II. Her Christian family welcomed anyone into their home, especially Jewish people whom Nazi soldiers hated for no other reason than that they were Jews. The Nazis arrested and put Jews in prison camps, where they suffered terribly and died.

The ten Booms prayed for the Jews, but they wanted to do more. They became part of something called "the Dutch underground." The family invited their Jewish friends to stay with them. If the Nazis ever came to the house, the ten Booms planned for their Jewish guests to hide in a secret place just big enough for six, behind a closet. Their plan worked for a while until the Nazis found out and arrested the ten Boom family. They were put in a prison camp and treated poorly. Some of Corrie's family died there, but she survived and was released. Corrie returned to the Netherlands and continued to help people in need. She even forgave the soldiers who were cruel to her.

Corrie spent the rest of her life traveling the world speaking about her experience with the Nazis and how faith and prayer steered her through that difficult time. She even wrote a book about it called *The Hiding Place*.

Corrie ten Boom often asked, "Is prayer your steering wheel or your spare tire?" Think about that. A steering wheel is used to guide a vehicle. Without it, that vehicle would be all over the road! A spare tire is a backup plan; it's there when you need it, but most of the time, you won't. So, when you think of Corrie, remember: like a steering wheel, you need prayer all the time—not just when you have trouble.

YOU MUST KEEP PRAYING. KEEP WATCHING! BE THANKFUL ALWAYS.
COLOSSIANS 4:2

MOTHER TeResA
{1910–97}

"Let Them See Jesus in Me"

Born to a Catholic family in Macedonia, Mother Teresa began her life as a little girl named Agnes. As a young girl, Agnes wanted to become a nun and help the poor—especially in India. At eighteen years old, she left home to train to work as a nun in India, and there she received a new name: Sister Mary Teresa.

While in India, Sister Mary Teresa first taught at a convent school in Calcutta. It was there that she received the name we know her by today—Mother Teresa. She soon felt Jesus telling her to leave the school and work directly with the poorest of the poor, so that's what she did. She went to the slums—extremely poor areas—of Calcutta where she cared for people who were sick, hungry, lonely, and forgotten. And every day, she prayed this prayer: "Dear Jesus. . .flood my soul with Thy spirit and love. Penetrate and possess my whole being so utterly that all my life may only be a radiance of Thine. Shine through me and be so in me that every soul I come in contact with may feel Thy presence in my soul. Let them look up and see no longer me but only Jesus. . . . Amen."

Others joined in helping with Mother Teresa's work. As more came, the group became known as the Missionaries of Charity. News of Mother Teresa's work spread around the world, and she became famous. Today she is remembered as one of the greatest and humblest Christians who ever lived.

Do you know what it means to be humble? Hint: reread Mother Teresa's daily prayer.

"aLL WHO Make THeMselVes GREAT WILL BE MADE HUMBLE,
BUT THOSE WHO Make THEMSELVES HUMBLE WILL BE MADE GREAT."
Luke 14:11 NCV

Teresa of Avila
{1515-82}

On-Fire Faith

If you had asked Teresa of Avila to describe her faith, she would have admitted that for a good while, forty years to be exact, it was only lukewarm—neither hot nor cold. It was quite average, really.

When Teresa was twenty-one years old, she joined a convent that was quite lenient. Teresa was allowed to have relationships with others outside the convent, and she was able to have her own belongings. These things allowed her to focus on things other than her devotion to God, which caused her faith to weaken.

One day while walking in the convent, Teresa noticed a statue of Jesus on the cross. She saw it in a way she hadn't before, and she felt Christ's powerful love for her. From that moment, Teresa's faith grew stronger. In fact, it became so strong that she gave up everything else. She put worldly things in the past and gave all her attention to the Lord and prayer.

Quiet prayer was important to Teresa. She said, "I would never want any prayer that would not make the virtues grow within me." God gave her a talent to lead, and Teresa started convents for women and monasteries for men where they could dedicate their lives to prayer and serving God.

Teresa devoted every day of her life to serving the Lord. She had a gift for understanding spiritual life and recorded her ideas about prayer and living for God. Even today, more than four hundred years later, her spiritual writing is read and studied. Teresa of Avila became a perfect example of a woman whose lukewarm faith became strong, on-fire faith.

What things are you focused on? Is there anything that distracts you from your relationship with God?

LEAD THEM IN THE RIGHT WAY SO THEY WILL HAVE STRONG FAITH.
TITUS 1:13

THÉRÈSE OF LISIEUX
{1873-97}

The Little Way

Oh, my God! I offer Thee all my actions of this day for the intentions and for the glory of. . .Jesus." Thérèse of Lisieux prayed this prayer every morning. She asked God to take everything she did that day and make it about Him.

When Thérèse said that prayer, she was living in a convent, away from the rest of the world. She had been there since age fifteen. It was what she wanted, to serve God as a nun and to pray for others. But it wasn't always a pleasant experience.

The convent was a cold place. Nuns only had what they absolutely needed and nothing else. Thérèse was the youngest nun in the convent. Some of the older nuns disliked her and called her "spoiled" because she had come from a middle-class family, and her father called her his "little princess." Life among these older women wasn't easy, and Thérèse sometimes imagined doing something else.

One day while reading the Bible, Thérèse realized that there were many different roles in the church. She read 1 Corinthians 13, and as she did, Thérèse felt her heart fill up with love. "Oh, Jesus," she prayed, "I have found my calling: my call is love."

From that day forward, Thérèse changed her attitude. Everything she did was about kindness and love. Even when others treated her badly, she responded with love. She called her acts of kindness "the Little Way." She did nothing grand or newsworthy, but in many little ways, whether through actions or prayers, Thérèse of Lisieux helped others.

Can you think of some little ways you can show others love and kindness? Ask God to help you with ideas.

LOVE TAKES EVERYTHING THAT COMES WITHOUT GIVING UP. LOVE BELIEVES ALL THINGS.
LOVE HOPES FOR ALL THINGS. LOVE KEEPS ON IN ALL THINGS.
1 CORINTHIANS 13:7

SOJOURNER TRUTH
{1797–1883}

The Traveler

Can you imagine being separated from your family and sold with a flock of sheep? That sort of life was not uncommon for African Americans when Sojourner Truth was a young girl.

Born into slavery, with the given name of Isabella, she found her own way to worship God. She spent time alone praying in the woods. She even built a temple made from brush in the woods, a skill she likely learned from her mother.

When Isabella was about thirty years old, the state of New York began allowing slaves the opportunity to leave their owners. Isabella made the decision to escape, because her owner didn't want to free her. She had no idea where she was going, but she prayed and trusted God to lead her in the right direction.

As a free woman, Isabella worked as a housekeeper and did missionary work with the poor in New York City. She had a very strong Christian faith and asked God to give her a new name. Isabella believed He wanted her to take the name Sojourner Truth.

Sojourner began traveling and preaching the truth from God's Word. And even though it wasn't socially acceptable at the time for women to voice their opinions in public, that didn't stop Sojourner Truth. She didn't think it was fair that African Americans and women didn't enjoy the same freedoms as white men. And she said so—and whenever she faced an obstacle, she prayed. Sojourner Truth worked hard to free the slaves in America and to gain equal rights for all women. When the Civil War ended and slavery became illegal in America, Sojourner Truth helped the newly freed slaves adjust to their new lives.

Sojourner Truth is remembered as a pioneer for civil rights and a great example of someone who put all her faith and trust in God. How can you be a positive example to others so they choose to trust and follow God too?

IT IS FOR FREEDOM THAT CHRIST HAS SET US FREE. STAND FIRM, THEN, AND DO NOT LET YOURSELVES BE BURDENED AGAIN BY A YOKE OF SLAVERY.
GALATIANS 5:1 NIV

HarrieT TUBMaN
{1820–1913}

Let My People Go!

If you know the story of Moses, you know that he led God's people, the Israelites, out of slavery in Egypt. Many years later, Harriet led *her* people, African Americans, out of slavery too. And that's how she came to be called the "Moses" of her people.

During Harriet's life, many kind and caring people wanted to help slaves escape through what was called the Underground Railroad. It wasn't a real railroad but was in fact a network of secret routes and passageways where runaway slaves would be safe to hide until they reached freedom in a state where slavery was illegal.

After years of abuse by her master, Harriet managed to escape from slavery. She traveled at night. "Come help me, Lord; I'm in trouble," she prayed. After a long journey and sheltering at the Underground Railroad houses along the way, Harriet reached freedom. But, for Harriet, it wasn't enough. She knew the way out, and so she returned—again and again—to help her family members and other slaves escape. Harriet remained persistent and courageous, risking her life to free others. "I prayed to God to make me strong and able to fight, and that's what I've always prayed for ever since," she said. Harriet trusted God for her safety while helping about three hundred slaves escape to freedom. Today she is remembered as the most famous leader of the Underground Railroad. Her story is taught in schools, and in 2020 her portrait will replace President Andrew Jackson's on the front of America's twenty-dollar bills.

Think about Harriet's courageous story. What do you think gave her strength not only to escape but also to go back and help others escape too?

. . . .

LIVE THIS Free LIFE BY LOVING aND HeLPING OTHers.
GALATIANS 5:13

MARY BALL WASHINGTON
{1707–89}

George Washington's Mom

A mother loves her kids no matter what, and that's how Mary Washington loved her son George. She loved him so much that sometimes her love was overbearing. Mary could be overprotective. When fifteen-year-old George wanted to join the navy, his mom wouldn't let him. Too dangerous! George loved his mother, but their relationship grew strained.

Mary had become an orphan at age thirteen. Maybe losing both her parents caused her to smother George with love. George understood what it felt like to lose a parent too. His dad died when George was only eleven. Mary's and her son's emotions over loss collided, and sometimes that caused stress.

When George grew up, he became the commander of the Continental Army during the American Revolutionary War—the war when American colonies fought for independence from Great Britain. His mother was at home in Fredericksburg, Virginia, worrying about him. There wasn't much she could do to help. So every day, she went to her favorite quiet spot, a rocky place with shade trees and climbing vines, and she prayed. Mary returned home, comforted and made strong by God's love.

After the war, and even after George became the first American president, their relationship remained tense. But that didn't diminish Mary's love for her son. They saw each other sometimes, and George helped her in her old age. We can only wonder if he realized how much his mother loved him and how often she prayed for him. She might have been overbearing, but Mary Ball Washington was a good mom.

There might be times when you don't get along with your parents, but don't allow that to separate you from them. Remember, they love you! God loves you too. Ask Him to help when you don't get along.

"I PRAYED FOR THIS BOY, AND THE LORD HAS GIVEN ME WHAT I ASKED OF HIM."
1 SAMUEL 1:27

SIMONE WEIL
{1909–43}

Searching for Truth

Simone Weil was born into a Jewish family in Paris. Her parents were agnostic—they had no opinion on whether God existed. When she became a teen, Simone felt like she didn't belong. She grew depressed. Her heart needed more. She longed for the truth—something, she wasn't sure what, that would bring beauty and goodness into her heart.

Simone hadn't read the Bible, but during her search for truth she discovered the Gospels. A verse in Matthew impressed her: "What man among you would give his son a stone if he should ask for bread?" (7:9). Simone had a heart for the poor and anyone who wasn't treated well. So this verse really meant something to her.

She became an activist for human rights, and that often got Simone into trouble. She was fired from teaching jobs because of her strong opinions. She went to work in factories to be among the poor, to be like those who were not treated well. Simone wanted to feel their pain.

The idea of Jesus and His suffering on the cross was one Simone could relate to. She began thinking more about Him. Then, while reading a poem about love, Simone felt Jesus come into her heart. She understood that He was the truth she searched for.

Simone asked God to empty her of everything she was. She asked Him to make her food for the poor. Simone had an intense personality. She could be somewhat of a drama queen! In her prayer, she asked God to make her lose all her senses and take over her mind. Regardless of the words she used, at that moment Simone welcomed Jesus, and truth, into her heart. She wanted to be more like Him.

....

JESUS SAID, "I AM THE WAY AND THE TRUTH AND THE LIFE.
NO ONE CAN GO TO THE FATHER EXCEPT BY ME."
JOHN 14:6

Susanna Wesley
{1669-1742}

A Mother Who Prayed

Susanna Wesley, mother of nineteen children, sometimes pulled her apron up over her head—which must have been a strange sight indeed! But her kids knew what this meant: *Leave Mom alone. She's busy talking with God.* So the children played, read, or studied around her while she prayed. Susanna's apron became a kind of worship tent where she could have some privacy to pray.

Susanna had to deal with a lot of hard things as a wife and mother. She gave birth to nine children who died when they were babies. Her husband, Samuel, a pastor, was not a good provider. In fact, his money problems were so bad that he ended up in jail. If that wasn't difficult enough, the Wesleys' house burned down not once but twice! After the second fire, it was necessary for the children to be separated and live in different homes until their house was rebuilt. This took two whole years!

You might think that dealing with such difficult things would make it hard for Susanna to be a good mom to her kids, but it didn't! Her strong faith and trust in God made her a great parent. She loved being with her children. And she even made it a priority to spend one-on-one time with each of her kids. In addition to running her busy household, she managed to educate the kids, teach them God's Word, and pray with them and for them.

Susanna trusted God to help her through every difficult circumstance she faced. And, most important, she continued to pray! Her conversations with God no doubt helped her get through each day with hope and faith in her heart. Do you rely on God to help you through hard times too?

· ·

HER CHILDREN SPEAK WELL OF HER. HER HUSBAND ALSO PRAISES HER,
SAYING, "THERE ARE MANY FINE WOMEN, BUT YOU ARE BETTER THAN ALL OF THEM."
PROVERBS 31:28-29 NCV

PHILLIS WHEATLEY
{1753-1784}

God Led the Way

Phillis Wheatley's story is an example of Romans 8:28: "We know that God makes all things work together for the good of those who love Him and are chosen to be a part of His plan."

The story begins with seven-year-old Phillis on a slave ship, kidnapped from her home in Africa and brought to America to be sold as a slave. Many slaves were treated badly by their owners, but Phillis would not be one of them. She was bought by John Wheatley to be a servant to his wife, Susanna. Mrs. Wheatley recognized how smart little Phillis was, so she and the two Wheatley children began teaching Phillis to read. That led to Phillis wanting to learn about many different things. The Wheatleys were a Christian family, so Phillis learned about Jesus and the importance of prayer. She gave her life to Jesus as her Savior and Lord and became a Christian.

By age ten, Phillis was reading books written in Greek and Latin and even translating them into English. She had a God-given gift to write, especially poetry, and the Wheatleys encouraged her, even allowing her to write instead of doing chores. Before long, Phillis's poems were published. She became the first African American and first US slave to publish a book of poems.

The Wheatleys freed Phillis from their ownership. As a free woman, she continued to write and sell her work. Many of her poems had a Christian theme.

"Oh Lord my God," she wrote in one of her prayer poems, "instruct my ignorance and enlighten my darkness. Thou art my King."

God had taken Phillis's very bad situation and worked it out for good. Phillis would face more struggles in her life, but she got through them all with prayer and help from her King.

AFTER YOU HAVE SUFFERED FOR AWHILE, GOD HIMSELF WILL MAKE YOU PERFECT. HE WILL KEEP YOU IN THE RIGHT WAY. HE WILL GIVE YOU STRENGTH.
1 PETER 5:10

Laura Ingalls Wilder
{1867–1957}

Laura's List

Do you know Laura Ingalls Wilder? She wrote a popular series of books about her life growing up in the days of American pioneers. The first book, *Little House in the Big Woods*, begins the story of Laura's lifetime of adventures and the hardships she and her family faced along the way.

The Ingalls were Christians. Praying, reading the Bible, and memorizing scripture were parts of their everyday lives. Laura wrote about their faith in her books. Laura also wrote a list of scriptures to read in different situations.

Laura's list (in her own words):

> *In facing a crisis read 46 Psalm*
> *When discouraged read 23 & 24 Psalm*
> *Lonely or fearful read 29 Psalm*
> *Planning budget St. Luke chapter 19*
> *To live successfully with others read Romans chapter 12*
> *Sick or in pain read 91 Psalm*
> *When you travel carry with you 121 Psalm*
> *When very weary read Matthew 11:28–30 and Romans 8:31–39*
> *When things are going from bad to worse read 2 Timothy 3rd chapter*
> *When friends go back on you hold to 1 Corinthians 13th chapter*
> *For inward peace the 14th chapter of St. John*
> *To avoid misfortune Matthew 7:24–27*
> *For record of what trust in God can do Hebrews 11*
> *If you are having to put up a fight—the end of Ephesians*
> *When you have sinned read 1 John 3:1–21*
> *and make Psalm 51 your prayer*

Laura's list can help you every day. Read Psalm 51 in your Bible, and while you read, think of Laura and all the other women you have met in this book. What have you learned from them about prayer?

* * *

"'THEN YOU WILL CALL UPON ME AND COME AND PRAY TO ME, AND I WILL LISTEN TO YOU.'"
JEREMIAH 29:12

THE WOMAN AT THE WELL
{JOHN 4:1-30}

Living Water

Jesus and His disciples were on a long walk to a place called Galilee. A small village in Samaria seemed the perfect place to rest. So, while His disciples went to buy lunch, Jesus sat by a well. A Samaritan woman came with a bucket to get water, and Jesus asked her for a drink.

Jews and Samaritans were not friendly toward each other. When Jesus, a Jew, asked the Samaritan woman for water, she said, "Who are *You* to ask *me*?" Jesus answered, "If you knew how generous God is and who I am, you would be the one asking—and I would give you living water."

Jesus knows everything. He knew the kind of life this woman led. She'd had five husbands, and now she was living with another man. But she wasn't eager for Jesus to know the truth. Jesus wanted her to live in a way pleasing to God. He wanted her to have *living water*, which meant believing in Him as the only way to get forever life in heaven.

Jesus told the Samaritan woman He knew all about her husbands and the other man. "It's not *where* you live that matters," Jesus said, "but *how* you live. God wants people who are truthful with themselves and also truthful with Him when they worship and pray."

"So you're a prophet," the woman said. "Well, someday the Christ is coming—the One who *really* knows everything. We'll see what *He* has to say."

"I am He," Jesus told her.

The Samaritan woman's story holds an important lesson in prayer. When you pray, be honest with Jesus. He wants truthfulness always. Don't be afraid. He already knows how you live. He will be quick to forgive if you ask.

. . . .

I CAN HAVE NO GREATER JOY THAN TO HEAR THAT MY CHILDREN ARE FOLLOWING THE TRUTH.
3 JOHN 4

THE WOMAN WHO NEEDED HEALING
{MARK 5:25–34; LUKE 8:43–48}

Just One Touch

The Bible tells a story about a woman who needed healing and displayed great faith—believing in something as perfect truth. We don't know her name, but we do know that she believed in Jesus with all her heart.

She had been sick for twelve years with a disease that made her bleed. The woman had seen many doctors, but none could help. Her illness became worse. On top of that, she had spent all her money on doctors. She had nothing left, and now she was desperate.

Jesus was coming! The woman heard He was traveling near where she lived. So she hurried there and saw a crowd following Him, pushing in from every side just to get near Him.

If only I can get close enough to touch His coat, I know I will be healed, the woman thought. So she pushed her way through the crowd, and when she was near enough, she touched the bottom of Jesus' tunic. As soon as she touched Him, the woman was healed.

Jesus stopped walking. "Who touched Me?" He asked. "I know someone touched Me because I felt power go out from Me."

The woman was so afraid that she shook. She knelt down in front of Jesus and told Him she believed that if only she touched Him, He would heal her.

Gentle Jesus said to her, "Daughter, your faith has healed you. Go in peace."

This woman's story happened many years ago. Today you don't have to touch Jesus to get His attention. Just pray with faith that Jesus can help with whatever you need. And if you need more faith, you can ask Him for that too. Jesus is always with you and ready to help.

THE FOLLOWERS SAID TO THE LORD, "GIVE US MORE FAITH."
LUKE 17:5

MORE GREAT BOOKS FOR COURAGEOUS GIRLS LIKE YOU!

100 Extraordinary Stories for Courageous Girls

Girls are world-changers! And this deeply inspiring storybook proves it! This collection of 100 extraordinary stories of women of faith—from the Bible, history, and today—will empower you to know and understand how women have made a difference in the world and how much smaller our faith (and the biblical record) would be without them.

Hardback / 978-1-68322-748-9 / $16.99

Cards of Kindness for Courageous Girls: Shareable Devotions and Inspiration

You will delight in spreading kindness and inspiration wherever you go with these shareable *Cards of Kindness*! Each perforated page features a just-right-sized devotional reading plus a positive life message that will both uplift and inspire your young heart.

Paperback / 978-1-64352-164-0 / $7.99

The Bible for Courageous Girls

Part of the exciting "Courageous Girls" book line, this Bible provides complete Old and New Testament text in the easy-reading New Life™ Version, plus insert pages featuring full color illustrations of bold, brave women such as Abigail, Deborah, Esther, Mary Magdalene, and Mary, mother of Jesus.

DiCarta / 978-1-64352-069-8 / $24.99